The
LETTERS
of
NAPOLEON
to
MARIE-LOUISE

From the portrait by Gérard

THE EMPRESS MARIE-LOUISE

The Letters of NAPOLEON to MARIE-LOUISE

With a Commentary by
CHARLES DE LA RONCIÈRE
Chief Custodian Bibliothèque Nationale of France

and an Introduction by
PHILIP GUEDALLA

With
31
Illustrations

HUTCHINSON & CO.
(Publishers) Ltd.
LONDON

Made and Printed in Great Britain at
The Mayflower Press, Plymouth. William Brendon & Son, Ltd.
1935

Introduction

by

Philip Guedalla

A HAPSBURG princess was the last and, perhaps, the most unlikely of Napoleon's conquests. For it was almost natural to find a successful military politician enthroned after a revolution as Emperor of the French and King of Italy, to watch his armies crossing Europe at a wild hand-gallop, and to see his relatives installed upon impromptu thrones in Holland, Spain, Westphalia, and Naples. Such things were only to be expected in the prevailing turmoil. But what demented prophet could reasonably have foretold that General Bonaparte would finally emerge from the confusion in the sedate capacity of son-in-law to the Emperor of Austria? That vision would have seemed to put an altogether undue strain upon credulity. Armed force might be unequal to the task of preventing him from marching armies into Berlin, Vienna, and Madrid. But the last sanctities of monarchy could still exclude a revolutionary Emperor from the most hallowed pages of the *Almanach de Gotha*. Could they? Not for long, it seemed; and that sublime impertinence was, in some ways, the most extravagant of all his conquests. Did it not marry a French gunner to a great-granddaughter of Maria Theresa? Or if that was not quite odd enough, the strange alliance wedded an ex-soldier of the Republic to a great-niece of Marie Antoinette, a commoner of forty to an Archduchess of eighteen. Like his other conquests, it vanished when the whole castle of his dreams collapsed before the dull reality of the Allies' advance in 1814; and in the next year the magician waved his wand in vain in a last effort to evoke it. For that conquest, like all the rest, slipped through his fingers. But whilst it lasted, it had been the supreme paradox of his career.

Their married life was an amazing contact of two worlds. It could not last. Indeed, the wonder is that it began at all. Ten years before, a little girl was playing soldiers with her brother in an Austrian nursery, and the villain of the piece was a ferocious effigy named Bonaparte, whose sinister original had driven all her father's soldiers out of Italy. This was an unpropitious opening. A little later she watched them packing; for Vienna was in danger, and the Court was relegated to the doubtful hospitality of distant provinces, while the Corsican intruder occupied her father's palace. Small wonder that she gleefully retailed fantastic prophecies of his approaching death. But when the prophecies came nearer and began to link his name with hers, her tone was still the same. "I pity the poor princess he chooses", wrote the destined lady of his choice. The nuptial menace grew; and now her tone was more submissive. "I resign my fate", she wrote, "into the hands of divine Providence. Providence alone knows how to make us happy. But if ill chance wills it so, I am ready to sacrifice my private happiness to the good of the State, convinced that true felicity is only to be found in doing our duty, even against our inclinations. I will not think about it any more, but my mind is made up, although it is a double and most painful sacrifice. Pray that it may never happen." It happened, all the same. For Austrian princesses were obedient instruments of Austrian policy; and Viennese statesmanship still respected the old exhortation,

Bella gerant alii: tu, felix Austria, nube.

Besides, she was above all things a dutiful daughter; and when the sacrifice was duly appointed, her father led a submissive Iphigenia to the altar.

Wedding-bells rung by diplomacy are rarely auspicious. But the bridegroom's intentions were not exclusively political, since he required an heir. So it was good to know that the bride's mother had twelve children, her grandmother sixteen, and her great-grandmother the same impressive total; and this encouraging arithmetic was the sound basis of Napoleon's courtship, as he turned hopefully towards the healthy Hapsburgs. A swift advance (on paper) from *Ma Cousine* to *Ma sœur* brought him to her side; one more Austrian was outmanœuvred; and she was soon *Ma bonne Louise*, the mother of his boy and the recipient of his daily letters from the front. It was a strange association; and the husband's correspondence survives to show how the queer bargain was interpreted by one party to it. His feeling for the little King of Rome appears in nearly every note, although his orders for the rapid issue of a portrait engraving of the boy with the appealing inscription, *Je prie Dieu qu'il sauve mon père et la France*, indicate that the propaganda value of a child's prayer was not beneath a father's notice. His tone with the young Empress was uniformly kind, and Napoleon appears at ease in the pleasant role of a *bon bourgeois*. But when the drift of Austrian policy grew threatening, he played the card which matrimony had put in his hand, dictating dutiful appeals for his young wife to write to "*papa François*". At the end, when all his hopes had crashed and he was relegated to an island off the coast of Italy, he seemed to pity her. Even his invincible egoism wavered before the prospect of a young woman's life with an ageing exile, and he tried to plan distractions for her on the mainland "when you tire of my Island of Elba and I begin to bore you, as I can but do when I am older and you still young". But she was not without her own distractions. For Elba never saw its Empress, and the strange partnership was over.

Of all the letters that he wrote to her less than half a dozen were previously known to the hungry investigations of Napoleonic scholars. The present collection contains more than three hundred, of which all but two are hitherto unpublished. It is a rich addition to his *personalia*. The serried volumes of his *Correspondance* contain twenty thousand documents to which he put his hand; and the subsequent researches of MM. Lecestre and Brotonne have added five thousand to the number, still further supplemented by an additional seven thousand pieces excavated by the industry of Colonel Picard and M. Tuetey from the Ministry of War. But a vast proportion of this immense accumulation consists of military and official matter, much of which was dictated. True, we already know how an ardent General could write to Josephine; but it is a welcome supplement to learn how he could write in later years to her successor.

A few nods in a London sale-room have transferred these precious scrawls from Austria to Paris, since a fitting gesture of the Third Republic acquired them for perpetual preservation beside their writer "*sur les bords de la Seine, au milieu de ce peuple français que j'ai tant aimé*".

Contents

Contents

List of Illustrations

List of Illustrations

The Letters of Napoleon to Marie-Louise

THE PURCHASE OF NAPOLEON'S LETTERS

EARLY in December, 1934, a sensational piece of news stirred the World of Letters to its depths. Over three hundred unpublished—nay, utterly unknown—letters from Napoleon I to the Empress Marie-Louise were about to be sold by auction in London. They bore upon the most pathetic periods of the Imperial epic, from the arrival in France of the Austrian Archduchess to the parting scenes at Fontainebleau.

The interest taken in them was heightened by the mystery of their origin. The catalogue drawn up for the sale merely stated that they were "the property of a nobleman to whom they have descended by inheritance". They were said to have been discovered by accident in an old Austrian castle.

Thus from an unexplored hiding-place there emerged a multitude of letters vainly sought for by the historians of the Emperor. Edouard

Cachot had journeyed to Bohemia, in quest of General Neipperg's papers, without finding them, and a historian, Frederic Masson, who had devoted a whole lifetime to the great Emperor, and built up a tremendous documentation about him, was driven, in his fine volume, *L'Impératrice Marie-Louise*, to this melancholy, to this painful admission: "I lack a vital element; the correspondence between Marie-Louise and Napoleon during the three years 1812, 1813 and 1814. They wrote to each other daily, often several times a day, and of these thousands of letters, apart from the official despatches, I have discovered but one, from the wife, and *five or six, from the husband*. For this fearful gap, which in all likelihood will never be bridged, I have made up to the best of my ability, but all too imperfectly."

And lo! in December, 1934, like a bolt from the blue, the almost inconceivable suddenly took shape: the gap was bridged. How happy the life-secretary of the French Academy would have been to handle that precious parcel of his idol's private letters! Alas, he passed away some dozen years too soon. But under the dome of the Institut there was another historian of Napoleon. M. Louis Madelin sounded a trumpet call in the public Press for the assistance of some generous patron. And the appeal was answered.

The Institut de France considered that it would be unseemly to allow this national patrimony to wander abroad. The Government—the Prime Minister, M. Flandin; the Minister of National Education, M. Mallarmé; and M. Herriot, who had held both those exalted posts, and who, moreover, had not forgotten the time when he wrote his *Life of Madame Récamier*, were all in favour of purchasing these letters of Napoleon's. A large sum of money was placed by the Government at the disposal of the Bibliothèque Nationale, upon which it rested to make up the balance.

From the very first, indeed, the Administrator General, M. Julien Cain, had taken in hand the work of rescue, called upon the Ministers, seen the journalists, co-ordinated the efforts of all. Were we to see the treasure escape us in the heat of the auction? For the last few years, fortunately, the Bibliothèque Nationale has enjoyed financial autonomy. A meeting of the Board was unobtrusively arranged for; and—an unheard-of occurrence in the annals of that great institution— the Bibliothèque Nationale was empowered to raise a loan with a view to contributing to the financial effort of the Government.

In the evening of December 17th, a telegram from London brought M. Julien Cain the news of a great victory. Napoleon's letters reverted to France once for all. They were about to find a home in that sanctuary, the "Réserve des Manuscrits" of the Bibliothèque Nationale.

* * *

These 318 letters from Napoleon I to Marie-Louise cover four years: the two months previous to the arrival of the future Empress at Compiègne, February to March, 1810; a short stay in the Nord department, in September and October, 1811; the Russian Campaign, May to December, 1812; the War in Germany, April to November, 1813; the Campaign in France, February to March, 1814; and the period subsequent to the fall of Paris, April to August 24th, 1814.

If the immense value of these documents is to be realized, they must be restored to their proper surroundings. It is necessary, also, to be acquainted with the reactions of the Empress to these letters of the Emperor, and as with one exception we are not in possession of her answers, we must needs have recourse to the private correspondence Marie-Louise continued to keep up with her friends of yore.

From the Portrait by Prud'hon.

MARIE-LOUISE

From the miniature by Chatillon,
in the Duke of Wellington's Collection.

THE EMPEROR NAPOLEON I.

I

THE MARRIAGE OF MARIE-LOUISE
(1810)

STRANGE as it may appear, the wife shortly to be repudiated by Napoleon, Josephine herself, was the first to whom it occurred to find someone to take her place with Napoleon.

It was at Malmaison, Josephine's home, that Countess Metternich, wife of the Austrian Chancellor, had the earliest inkling of this plan, of which she promptly informed her husband on January 3rd, 1810. Josephine had with her at the time her son, Eugène de Beauharnais, and her daughter Hortense, Queen of Holland. The mother had broached the subject to her children, and the impetuous Eugène had been prompt to translate the idea into action.

"You know we are all Austrians at heart", Queen Hortense declared to Countess Metternich. "But what you would never guess is that my brother was bold enough to suggest to the Emperor that he should ask for your Archduchess."

Developments followed in swift succession. On January 10th, the Paris Officialty declared null and void the marriage between Napoleon and Josephine. This decision disarmed the opposition of the clergy to a marriage between a *divorcé* and a Roman Catholic Princess.

But would the Emperor's choice fall upon a Roman Catholic Princess? There was a diversity of opinion on the subject. A Princess Royal of England, Charlotte-Augusta? The Russian Imperial Princess, Anna Pavlovna? The Queen of Holland, Hortense, who would previously have divorced her husband?—No, it was Josephine's choice who carried the day: the Archduchess Marie-Louise-Léopoldine-Caroline-Lucie, one of the thirteen children Marie-Louise de Bourbon-Sicile had borne to Emperor Francis the Second of Germany, and the First of Austria. Having been born on December 12th, 1791, Marie-Louise was eighteen years old.

Already, in Vienna, there was talk both of the Emperor's divorce and of his projected remarriage. Such an alliance would mark the end of an exhausting struggle which had been kept up by Austria against Napoleon since 1796, and which had already cost her Lombardy, Brisgau and the left bank of the Rhine, under the Treaty of Campo-Formio; Tuscany, at Lunéville; the Venetian States and Tyrol, at Presburg; Carniola, Carinthia, Friuli, Dalmatia and Galicia, at Schönbrünn.

"I am only sorry for the poor Princess he will choose", writes the Archduchess Marie-Louise, on January 10th, to her friends, Countess Collendo and Victoire de Poutet, the Countess's daughter by a former marriage: "for I am sure I shall not be the victim of politics . . . Napoleon is too much afraid of a refusal and too bent upon doing us further harm to venture upon such a request; and Papa is too kind to coerce me in so important a matter". "I know that in Vienna they are already marrying me to the great Napoleon", she writes on January 23rd to her young friend Victoire. "If such a thing should come to pass, I verily believe I should be the only one not to rejoice at it."

"*Souvent femme varie et bien fol est qui s'y fie*", as Napoleon was to learn at his cost. To bring this girl of eighteen to approve of a man of forty, for all the glory with which he was crowned, Metternich urged reasons of State. Napoleon, informed by his Ambassador, Otto, of Marie-Louise's appearance of resplendent health, conceived the hope that she would bear him an heir. He declared himself without further ado.

And at this point the letters purchased by the Bibliothèque Nationale throw a remarkable light on Napoleon's amorous psychology. The only one hitherto published in his *Correspondence* is that dated February 23rd, 1810, a copy of which is filed in the State Archives, as having constituted an official demand in marriage.

Ma Cousine
The brilliant qualities that distinguish your person have inspired us with the desire to serve and honour you by approaching the Emperor, your Father, with the request that he shall entrust to us the happiness of your Imperial Highness. May we hope that the feelings which prompt us to take this step will be

acceptable to you? May we flatter ourselves with the belief that you will not be guided solely by the duty of obeying your Parents? Should the feelings of your Imperial Highness be partial to us, we would cultivate them so carefully and strive so constantly to please you in every way, that we flatter ourselves with the hope of succeeding some day in winning your regard; such is the aim we would fain encompass, and in respect of which we beg your Highness to favour us.

Whereupon, my Cousin, we pray God to have you in His Holy and Worthy keeping.

Your good Cousin

NAPOLEON

RAMBOUILLET 23 *Feb*. 1810

And to his "cousin" he sent his likeness by Marshal Berthier. Of Napoleon at the age of forty, at the time of his second marriage, his secretary, Baron Fain, has given us the following outline. Of small stature—five feet two—but well set up, a rather short neck, and perhaps already a trifle pot-bellied, of soft fibre and heavy lymph, cheeks of a dead white, a full face, a round head, a broad, high forehead, blue-grey eyes, a gentle glance, a finely-chiselled nose, a graceful mouth and fine teeth—there was nothing displeasing about the flat-haired man of forty. His eyesight was not of the best and often compelled the use of an opera-glass, which he invariably had about him. "The regularity of his features often imparted to him, when at work or preoccupied, a hint of sternness; but in the easy-going conditions of private life, his smile again took on great amiability. More quickly than any other person's, moreover, his expression changed under the sway of his emotions. From the same glance, so caressing just before, there suddenly came forth flashes of lightning."

One thing about him of which Marie-Louise was not apprized by his first missive was his hand-writing, for he had had recourse to the pen of a secretary. While dictating, he would walk up and down the whole time, with slow and measured tread, occasionally plucking at the facings of his sleeve.

But love very soon induced him to submit to the torture of writing with his own hand "a medley of unconnected and illegible signs. The words lacked half their proper number of letters", writes Baron Méneval, his secretary. "He was unable to read over what he himself had written, or he would not take the trouble of doing so. When asked for an explana-tion he would snatch up his rough draft and tear it to pieces or throw it in the fire. His short notes, or the few lines he chanced to write, which called for no particular concentration of mind, were generally free from mistakes in spelling, save as regards certain words in which the same mistakes invariably occur—*gabinet*, *Gaffarelli*, *enfanterie*, reminiscences of his mother tongue."

It was in a letter from Paris, dated February 25th, 1810, that Marie-Louise had occasion for the first time to become acquainted with that uncouth handwriting.

Madame ma Sœur

The successful issue of my request to His Majesty the Emperor, your Father, to be joined to you in marriage, is a most precious token of the esteem and regard in which he holds me. I highly appreciate the consent you yourself bestow upon a union which fills me with the most heartfelt joy and which will embellish the whole of my life. I look forward with the liveliest impatience to the moment when its conclusion will be in sight. I appreciate, above all, in his bond, the care I am determined to take to make you happy; my wishes, in this respect, are all the more sincere in that my own happiness will be vitally bound up with yours. I have instructed the Prince de Neufchâtel, my Ambassador Extraordinary and Plenipotentiary, to deliver to you my portrait. I beg you to accept it as a token of the feelings which are graven in my heart and which will remain unalterable. I am, Madam my Sister, your most affectionate brother.

NAPOLEON

PARIS 25 *Feb.* 1810

The style of address to be adopted in respect of Her Imperial Highness was not yet settled in his mind, for the first letter is headed "Ma Cousine", the second "Madame ma Sœur", and the third, dated from the Tuileries, February 25th, "Ma Sœur", a strange form of address to apply to a Princess whom he wished to make his wife.

Later, indeed, once the marriage was decided upon, he used the term "Madame", before addressing her in a homely way as "Ma bonne Louise".

Ma Sœur

I hear how perfect you were, all the trust you show in me on this occasion is very precious to me I feel the need to tell you so without delay. Would you be kind enough to appreciate all I feel on hearing everybody praise so highly your person and the eminent qualities which cause you to be worshipped by my peoples? As for me, Madam, I would fain place at your feet my homage, my hopes and all the tender compliments enclosed in my heart. If the happiness of Your Imperial Highness is to depend upon the genuineness of my affection, no one will be happier than you: this idea pleases me and is very sweet.

Your good Brother

NAPOLEON

FROM THE TUILERIES 25 *Feb.* 1810

On March 1st, a letter from the Emperor was sent off which "will reach you after the celebration of our marriage", wrote Napoleon, who already spoke of the Archduchess as "Your Majesty". It was by proxy, of course, that Napoleon, on March 11th, married Marie-Louise of Austria in the Capuchin Chapel of the Hofburg, at Vienna. And he accredited to her household, to accompany her to France, Marshal Berthier, Prince de Neuchâtel, and his own sister Caroline Bonaparte, Murat's wife and Queen of Naples.

Madame

This letter will be handed to you after the celebration of our marriage. No single letter reaches me from Vienna that does not speak admiringly of your noble qualities. I look forward with the utmost eagerness to finding myself in presence of Your Majesty. Were I to give way to my desires, I would ride off without more ado and be at your feet before any one knew I had left Paris; but it is not to be. The Prince de Neufchâtel will receive your orders during your journey. My sister Caroline wishes to keep you company; give her a friendly welcome, she is very kind to me. I have but one thought and that is to know what may be agreeable to you. The care of pleasing you, Madame, will be the most constant and the sweetest concern of my life.

NAPOLEON

1 *March*

Love, they say, is blind. This was not the case with Marie-Louise when she opened the Imperial missive. H.I.H. the Archduchess, stated a communication from Vienna, dated March 9th, and published in the *Gazette de France*, has received a letter written by H.M. the Emperor of the French himself, in which he thanks her in the most moving terms for leaving her august father, her family and her country for his sake. H.M. is known to write extremely fast, which often makes his handwriting difficult to read for those who are not used to it. But the Archduchess Marie-Louise, much to the surprise of all those with her, read the letter as fast as if it had been in her own handwriting.

The demand in marriage was solemnly presented in March. Napoleon's Ambassador Extraordinary, Marshal Berthier, received on alighting from his coach by the Grand Marshal of the Court, was led into the Throne room, where the Emperor Francis sat under a canopy, surrounded by his family and his attendants. The demand was granted, and Marie-Louise received permission to hang Napoleon's portrait, delivered on a cushion by a horseman of the Embassy, round her neck.

In his happiness the Emperor associates his people, for whom this girlish bride will be "a loving mother". And in a few words straight from the heart he sympathizes with the regrets she must feel at leaving Vienna and her father's palace: "All your troubles are my troubles."

Madame
      I hope Your Majesty will receive this letter at Braunau, and even beyond. I count the moments. The days seem long. It will be thus until I have the happiness of welcoming you. My people share my impatience. I have told them you would be a tender mother for the French; you will find in them, Madame, children that cherish you. I hope you are fully satisfied of the genuineness of my affections. You will find nothing wanting in this respect, but I am most anxious to hear that you share them. Believe me, there is no one in the world more attached to you or more determined to love you than myself.

NAPOLEON

10 *March* 1810

Madame
      Lauriston tells me of all the kind things you have been good enough to say to him, and speaks of Your Majesty in terms which, while adding no whit to the high conception I have formed of your noble qualities, I nevertheless keenly appreciate. You have by this

time left Vienna. I am alive to the regrets you must feel; all your sorrows are my sorrows. I very often think of you, I would fain guess what is of a nature to please you and to deserve your heart. Allow me to hope, Madame, that you will help me to win that heart, the whole of your heart. This hope is a necessity for me and makes me happy.　　　　　NAPOLEON

15 March 1810

On receipt of the portrait of Marie-Louise, which "bears the stamp of a lofty soul", Napoleon is more and more inflamed. To the General favoured by Fortune, a daughter of the Cæsars brings the tribute of her freshness.

The most eminent Viennese masters have worked on the portrait of the Princess. The famous Lampi, whom no modern artist is held to have equalled in the matter of perfect colouring, used all his talent for the purpose of recording her features in an oil-painting. And Gérard, the miniaturist, also took her as a model.

Madame
　　　　　I have received your portrait. The Empress of Austria has been considerate enough to have it given to me. I seem to see in it the reflection of that beautiful soul which makes you so dear to all who know you, and justifies all the hopes I have placed in Your Majesty. You will love, Madame, a spouse whose claims will never be based on anything but your trust and the feelings of your heart. I presume you are very close to France by this time and I await you with much impatience.　　　　　NAPOLEON

PARIS 20 *March*

We are not given the letters from Marie-Louise which, to quote his secretary, Baron Méneval, "delighted" the Emperor. These replies were written in good French and the feelings expressed in them were marked by delicacy and moderation; perhaps the Queen of Naples had something to do with this.

With a view to rendering himself more attractive, the Emperor, at the suggestion of the Queen of Fashion, Princess Pauline, had ordered a fancy coat to be made for himself, which was adorned with embroidery, but in the opinion of his secretary the white stock made him look stiff, whereas in uniform, with a black stock, his appearance was one of easy distinction. Napoleon almost immediately discarded the obnoxious garment and reverted to the green jacket of a rifleman of the Guard, or to the blue coat with white facings which he wore on Sundays.

On March 13th, Marie-Louise set out from Vienna, saluted on her departure by a salvo of the whole of the artillery, and the ringing of all the church bells, with troops lining the road, a Division of Cuirassiers riding in front of the procession. The Grand Master of the Palace, the Grand Master of the Post, the Grand Mistress, the Chamberlains, the Ladies of the Palace, in coaches drawn by six or eight horses, formed an imposing retinue.

At St. Polten, where she was to put up for the night, her father, the Emperor Francis, and her stepmother had come in the strictest incognito to wish her good-bye. What tears the poor child

27

now shed at the thought of leaving her relatives! The sound of her sobs did not fail to reach Napoleon.

* * *

From the day he knows himself to be her husband by proxy—the Archduke Charles had been entrusted with the proxy—Napoleon followed the journey of Marie-Louise day by day, hour by hour, with amorous solicitude.

At Braunau, on the frontier, a carefully appointed hut had been erected. Here, under a canopy, an arm-chair upholstered in gold awaited Marie-Louise; and near by there was a table with a green cloth for the plenipotentiaries to sign upon. For here Marie-Louise said good-bye to Austria, and to her beloved governess, the Countess Leczinska. The Grand Master of the Court, Prince Trautmansdorf, handed over the Empress to the care of Marshal Berthier, Prince de Neuchâtel, assisted in the capacity of secretary by Count de Laborde. Thereupon there came into the room, to take the place of the Austrian household, the Duchess of Montebello as lady-in-waiting, and Count de Beauharnais as knight of honour.

The King of Bavaria had sent his Master of the Ceremonies. At every halt in one of his cities two hundred guns were fired. At Munich, on March 17th, all the troops, the whole of the National Guard were assembled under arms; guns, bells and shouts of joy hailed the appearance of Marie-Louise. The lordly mansions, the Town Hall, the public buildings, the squares are adorned

28

with emblems; in these, the name of Napoleon is intertwined with that of Louise, and the Lion of Bavaria rests in peace between the French and the Austrian Eagles; the warriors of the three nations touch glasses. Such is the entrancing picture drawn by the *Gazette de France* of the entry of Marie-Louise into Munich. It is to all this Napoleon refers in his notes of welcome.

Madame

     I have received your letter of the 18th. I am greatly concerned to hear that Your Majesty is slightly indisposed. I beg and pray you to be careful of a health that is so precious to me; it is no longer yours, Madam, since you have been good enough to give me certain claims upon it, on which I base my happiness. Caroline sends me charming accounts which fill me with the most tender feelings. I had a very fine day's shooting, yesterday, and yet I found it insipid. All that is not you no longer interests me. I feel that I shall have nothing left to wish for when once I have you here. This letter will be handed to you by Field Marshal the Duke of Istria, who is in command of my household cavalry and to whom I have entrusted the governorship of Nancy during your passage. A Chamberlain of the Emperor's has handed me letters from Vienna that are very amiable; I do not propose to answer them before having seen you, so as to express thanks for the happiness of having you, Louise, who shall constantly be the object of my most tender feelings. A thousand regards at your feet, and a sweet kiss upon your charming hand.

NAPOLEON

23 *March* 1810

Madame

I hear you have dispensed with the services of your Governess, in order to show yourself to my people surrounded solely by Frenchwomen. I approve and I am very grateful for this while at the same time it makes me sad. This further sacrifice added to that of your father and of your family will again have made your heart bleed. However, Madame, you will not lay the blame upon your husband; it was not in his power to spare you these painful moments, which are in the nature of things. I should be inconsolable were you to think I could ever be so tactless as not to spare you any sorrow it was in my power to spare you. Please be so very kind as to write me a few words on the subject. I am greatly concerned lest I should have incurred your displeasure. Be sure my heart fully appreciates your sacrifices; should all its tenderness and its constant and tender love avail to repay you, you have nothing to wish for. Laborde, who has just arrived from Vienna, tells me you have cried a great deal since leaving St. Polten; you were also fretting at Munik [Munich]. This vexes me, for I want Louise to have none but pleasant days, as beautiful and agreeable as she is herself. Caroline informs me that you very much wish to know what can make me happy. I will tell you that secret myself, Madame. It will appear simple to you and yet it is perfectly true. *Be really happy at our marriage.* When you feel inclined to give way to sorrow, when you feel worried, say to yourself: the Emperor will be deeply grieved, for he can be satisfied and happy only through the happiness of his Louise.

Your
NAPOLEON

COMPIÈGNE 23 *March* 1810

The King of Bavaria had joined the procession, which at Stuttgart received the addition of another king. The capital of Wurtemberg was illuminated throughout on March 20th. Opposite the Royal Palace there stood a temple with the names of Napoleon and Marie-Louise shining forth in letters of fire on its pediment, and below, the hymeneal altar. In the evening, after dinner, a performance was given of Ritter's opera *The Judgment of Solomon*, the recitative of which had been composed by the Kapelmeister Danzi. From Stuttgart, Marie-Louise sent a note to Napoleon.

Will France outshine the countries beyond the Rhine? As to Strasburg, Napoleon is somewhat uneasy. But from the Kehl bridge to the Imperial Palace, the ovations were continuous; a fountain formed a symbolic bow of alliance; on foot, on horseback, in carts decked with flowers, the peasants file past uninterruptedly in local dress; a banquet for the soldiers at the Robertsau; another for the Empress and her retinue at the house of the Prefect Lezay-Marnésia. Napoleon could make his mind easy, the rejoicings were complete. One of her pages delivered to Marie-Louise, together with a bunch of flowers, the following letter.

Madame

I had just sent off the letter I wrote to you yesterday when I received Your Majesty's letter from Stuttgart. You write such sweet things and give me such touching assurances that my heart is deeply

31

moved. The letters of the Prince de Neufchâtel and Caroline fill me with tenderness towards you and increase my impatience; how happy I shall be to see you and tell you of all my affection for you! The telegraph informed me yesterday that you had caught cold. I do beg you to take care of yourself. I went shooting this morning and am sending you the first four pheasants I shot as a royalty that is but due to the Queen of all my most secret thoughts. Why am I not in the place of the page taking the oath of allegiance, with one knee on the ground, and my hands in yours? Receive it in imagination, at least; just as I, in imagination, cover your beautiful hands with kisses. This evening, you are still at Lunéville. To-morrow you will be seeing Prince Schwarzenberg and Countess Metternich; I thought their visit would please you. I long to hear whether you liked our good city of Strasburg.

Adieu, Madame, you speak of me, you think of me, and this idea is a very charming one for me. More-over, it is but fair, for I think of you very often, Louise.

Your

NAPOLEON

COMPIÈGNE 24 *March* 1810

Napoleon came to meet the Empress at the Palace of Compiègne. Looking back to the ceremony at Notre-Dame, when he placed the crown on the brows of Josephine, who knelt before him, he ordained the procedure of his first interview with Marie-Louise. Their Majes-ties were to meet at a spot two leagues from Soissons, where a tent had been put up; the Empress was to bend low before him, but before she knelt, the Emperor was to have raised her up.

From the picture by E. B. Garnier.

THE WEDDING PROCESSION

The Emperor Napoleon I and Marie-Louise of Austria,
April 2nd, 1810.

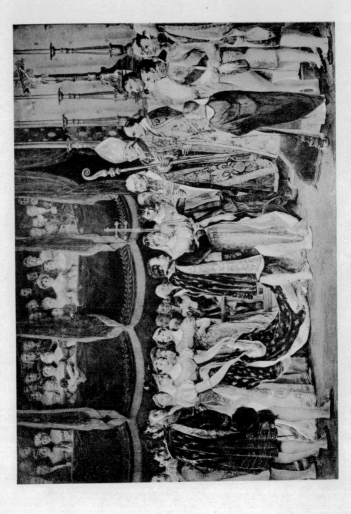

THE MARRIAGE OF NAPOLEON AND MARIE-LOUISE
The Louvre.   April 2nd, 1810.

His impatience, and likewise the rain, altered these arrangements. Setting out hastily in a light carriage on March 27th, with Murat, King of Naples, he met the daughter of the Emperor Francis at the village of Courcelles. "Madame", he said to her, "it gives me great pleasure to meet you". And entering the coach he returned with her to Compiègne, arriving there at ten o'clock in the evening.

The civil marriage was celebrated at Saint-Cloud on April 1st. The next day, the Emperor and Empress made a solemn entry into Paris by the Etoile gate, passing under the yet unfinished Arc-de-Triomphe. Glorious sunshine lit up the entrancing spectacle of the procession advancing in the midst of a huge crowd towards the Tuileries Palace. An altar had been erected in the Salon d'Apollon at the Louvre. Here, in presence of the Queens of Spain, Holland and Westphalia, of the Princess Elisa Baciocchi, and Pauline Borg-hèse, bearing the train of the Empress, Cardinal Fesch, Grand Almoner, gave the nuptial blessing to the bride and bridegroom. And at night the whole of Paris, monuments, churches, towers, domes, palaces, mansions and private houses, were lit up by thousands of lights. By the magnificence of its wedding gifts the capital had risen to the occasion: silver-gilt plate for the Emperor, a silver-gilt toilet set, complete with arm-chair and cheval-glass for the Empress.

On April 5th, in a gilt berlin, upholstered inside with white silk, the Imperial pair drove to "another Schönbrünn", Compiègne.

Was Marie-Louise, the "decent sort who kisses one full on the lips", to quote her new cousin, Elisa Baciocchi, happy? For an answer to so indiscreet a question, turn to the letter written by the Empress, on April 24th, to one of the friends of her childhood, Victoire de Poutet:

"Dear Victoire, I am very sincerely grateful to you for your good wishes on the occasion of my marriage. Heaven has answered them. May you soon enjoy such happiness as I myself feel."

II

THE JOURNEY OF THE IMPERIAL PAIR IN THE NORTH OF FRANCE

THE policy of France was weighed down by the Napoleonic conception of the Continental Blockade against England. Set up by the Berlin Decree of November 21st, 1806, the so-called "System" had alienated from the Emperor his own brother, Louis, King of Holland, whose shipowners were ruined thereby and who ultimately abdicated on July 1st, 1810. Eight days later, Holland was annexed to France. Hence Napoleon's journey in the North of France.

England's reply to the Continental Blockade was a naval blockade. As soon as he reached Boulogne, on September 19th, 1811, Napoleon was faced with the sight of the British cruisers on guard. This provoked him beyond measure. He took to a dinghy in company of Post Captain Le Coat de Saint-Haouen, and on the 21st, by his orders, the flotilla of gunboats under Rear-Admiral Baste gave chase to the enemy cruisers. The two following letters, dated from Boulogne, refer to this:

Ma chère Louise

I arrived at 9 o'clock in the evening. I stayed 2 hours at Montreuil to order some works. I had frightful heat and a great deal of dust. I want you to go and sleep at Valenciennes, leaving at 4 o'clock in the morning, and the second day at Laeken. You would be tired out covering the distance in one day; the dust would give you a nasty cough. So do as I tell you. I hope you will have been reasonable and that you are sound asleep by this time. It is midnight. I am going to bed. Adieu, mon amie. A very tender kiss.

NAP.

BOULOGNE 19 [*Sept.* 1811] 11.30 *p.m.*

Ma bonne Louise

I wrote to you last night. I have this instant received your letter, which gives me great pleasure, because it is kind, just as you are. I have been at sea all day long; I had the English cruisers chased at Cayeu (?). The weather was magnificent. My health is very good. Pray take care of yourself. You know the dust (?) and the heat disagree with you. I am remaining here to-morrow, for I have lost all hope of learning naval manners. Adieu, Louise. You are quite right to think of him whose only hope is in you.

NAP.

BOULOGNE 21 [*Sept.* 1811] 8 *p.m.*

Marie-Louise, also, travelled northwards, bringing her graciousness to bear where Napoleon more particularly bent the eye of the master. She entered Brussels at 1 a.m. on September

22nd, to the sound of artillery salvos, along streets streaming with lights. As beflowered as an altar, Laeken Palace, in which a room with pink hangings had been prepared for her, was a regular "Fairy Palace", to quote an eye-witness. And at night, when Marie-Louise appeared in an open carriage, bands struck up as a salute.

At Saint-Gudule she admired the stained-glass windows and tapestries of the Cathedral. In a lace factory, Mademoiselle Noens presented her with a design in which the Genius of Trade was shown leaning upon the Imperial Eagle to strike down the Monster of Discord. The nights at Brussels were all enchantment: a ball given by the city, a ball in honour of Pauline Bonaparte, Princess Borghese, performance at the Opera of *Maison à vendre*, etc. . . .

From Boulogne, passing through Calais, Napoleon reached Ostend. He would not hear of any reception. He was the Artillery Officer on a round of inspection; the preceding years he had found disturbing conditions. "At Dunkerque, the engineers are in a lamentable state." Elsewhere "the gunboats of the Navy are not exercised". He proceeded to enquire personally into the state of the fortifications and that of the fleet. At Ostend, with an eye to the evil consequences of the naval blockade, he promises to do all he can to promote the exportation of French wines and Lyons silks. Yet there is no sign of such concerns in the love-letters written to the Empress.

Ma bonne Louise

I have received your letter of 7ber 20th. I spent all day viewing my troops. I am leaving and shall be at Ostend to-morrow. I shall be with you at the time I mentioned. I am glad to see it has rained a little to-day. You will have no dust. The journey will be less fatiguing for you. I am anxious to hear you are at Laeken in good health; I hope you will like the Belgians and that you will enjoy yourself while with them. You know how I love you; you are mistaken in thinking any matters I have in mind can detract one whit from the sentiments I bear you. Adieu, mon amie. To-morrow I shall be with you. I will write you from Ostend.

23 *Sept.* 1811

Mon amie

I have received your letter from Laeken. The dust must have done you a great deal of harm. I shall spend the night on board my fleet; I am in very good health. As you see, we shall soon be together again. Tell me whether you were pleased with the people at Brussels and whether you are comfortable at Laeken. Enjoy yourself and take care of your health; the dust must have fatigued you sadly. Adieu, ma bonne Louise, tout à toi.

NAPOLEON

[OSTEND] 24 [*Sept.* 1811] 7 *a.m.*

Leaving Ostend on horseback, Napoleon proceeded to Zwyn. Here he found nothing but a fishing smack to take him across. This he boards, in the pouring rain, attended by Caulaincourt, Count Lobau and two chasseurs of the Guard.

On landing in the Isle of Cadzand: "First of all, Gentlemen", he observes to the officers of Breskens, "a good fire; I am drenched to the skin". Then, turning to the owner of the smack:

"Let us see, old tar, what is your charge for bringing us across? It is my treat."

"Three shillings a head, Sir. Will that be too dear?"

"How much does that amount to?"

"A 'plaquette' (about 2d.) less than a florin"— about two French livres.

"That is not enough. Give him a hundred napoleons! And in addition, so that you may not forget me, you shall have an annuity of 300 livres." What a fine anecdote to tell Marie-Louise ! Yet the note he sent her makes no mention of this Imperial generosity.

Mon amie

      I arrived last night rather fatigued at Breskens. I rode all the way from Ostend. I am going to view the forts I am having built. I shall sleep on board my squadron, which is lying here. I was drenched, it is still raining. My health is excellent and I had no news from you yesterday. I hope you are well and that you like Brussels. Adieu, Louise. Keep well and love your faithful husband.

                                          N.

BRESKENS 24 *7ber* [1811]

After inspecting the Fort Napoleon and the Fort du Centre in the Isle of Cadzand, he joined the squadron and hoisted his pennant on the

Charlemagne at 1 p.m. on September 24th. Then, starting with the *Anversois*, he visited all the ships of the line and had them manœuvred in his presence.

On board the *Charlemagne* were Vice-Admirals Ganteaume and Missiessi and Rear-Admiral Ruisch. The Emperor, who was a good sailor but inveighed against the rolling of the ship, made a point of displaying his knowledge of naval affairs while conversing with his guests after dinner. And so well informed did he prove to be that Ruisch, in his amazement, leaned over towards Ganteaume and asked him in a whisper: "Where on earth did His Majesty learn our trade?"

"Gentlemen", said the Emperor at the close of the conversation, "I have nothing but praise to bestow on you. I was impressed with the excellent appearance of the crews, and I wish to give them tokens of my satisfaction. This is a family gathering ; let us settle our accounts. Admiral Missiessy, who are the worthy people under your orders who distinguished themselves most?"

"Sire, every one of the officers."

"Tut, tut, you are all like that—given to spoil your subordinates. We are not concerned with the officers, just now; a commission in the Navy is quite enough to keep a man satisfied for a long time."

"Your Majesty is quite right", exclaimed Ganteaume. "I would recommend pilot Thomas, of Brest."

"And I, pilot Mathieu Amadis, of Flushing",

added Rear-Admiral Ruisch. And the bestowal of a warrant for an annuity of a thousand crowns to the brave Dutch seaman, who had already been given the ribbon of the Legion of Honour, was effected solemnly in the presence of the whole crew assembled on the main deck.

The night was used by Napoleon "in bringing the portfolios up to date", for he had with him the Minister of Marine and the Home Minister. Many decrees are dated September 25th and 26th, 1811, on board the *Charlemagne*. Two of his notes to Marie-Louise bear the same date.

I have just received your letter of the 24th, *mon amie*, on rising to do my correspondence. It is blowing very hard, the sea is rather rough, but I feel none the worse for it. I viewed the whole of my squadron yesterday, ship by ship. I had 24 of the biggest and that are in very good condition. I am going to have them manœuvred to-day if the wind abates somewhat, though I am visiting Flushing and pushing on to Antwerp. I have written Estr . . . (?) to forward 30,000 livres to you for your private purse. You may order or purchase 100,000 livres worth of lace at Brussels. I will have them paid for. Adieu, ma bonne Louise. I am glad to know you are in good health.

ON BOARD THE "CHARLEMAGNE", IN THE ROADS OF THE SCHELDT, 25*th*, 3 *a.m.* [25 *Sept.* 1811].

N.

Ma bonne Louise
Yesterday was windy. Great guns. I am without news of you. I was 2 days without being able to communicate with the mainland; the sea was rough.

I shall remain on board for another day to have the squadron manœuvred. The day after to-morrow I shall proceed to Flushing and lastly to Antwerp. I hope to hear this evening you are in very good health and that you like Brussels. I was not seasick, though many of the Household were. Adieu, mon amie. I am glad to think I shall be seeing you soon.

NAP.

ON BOARD THE "CHARLEMAGNE" [26 *Sept.* 1811]. 6 *p.m.*

Reaching his yacht at Flushing, on September 27th, the Emperor inspects the defensive works like a man who knows his business, the forts of Montebello, Saint-Hilaire and Ramekens, the caponiers, the couronnes, the cavaliers. And he dictated the result of his observations to the War Minister Clarke, Duc de Feltre: "There are but few mortars on platforms at Flushing. For continuous firing, Gomer mortars are sufficient. But for keeping enemy ships at a distance, mortars on platforms are more suitable." Between whiles, he writes:

Ma bonne Louise

I have just landed at Flushing. Leaving the *Charlemagne*, I embarked on my yacht at 5 o'clock in the morning. I reached Flushing at 8 o'clock, in good health. I am now going to finish viewing my fortifications and naval works ... I have received no letters from you to-day ... with the Princess Pauline and the Queen of Naples, who are arriving to-day as you will see. I am longing to see you. I hope it cannot be delayed much longer. I love you. Adieu, ma Louise.

NAP.

27 [*Sept.* 1811] 7 *p.m.*

THE HEIR

Napoleon presenting the baby King of Rome to
the Dignitaries of the Empire.

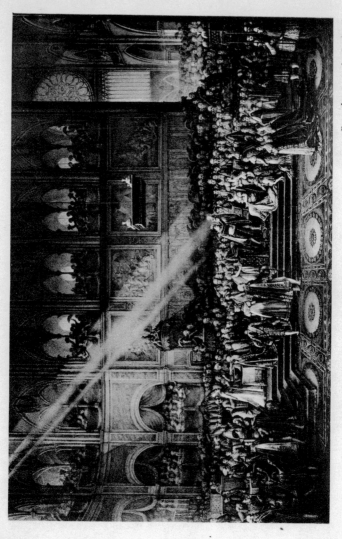

From the picture by Goubaud.

THE BAPTISM OF THE KING OF ROME

Showing Napoleon holding his baby son

Mon amie

I have received your letter. The Princess Pauline is so ill that she is to be pitied. I was in the saddle all day long yesterday. I shall leave to-morrow; I hope to see you soon, which gives me great pleasure. Adieu, ma bonne Louise. You are in good health, I trust. Tout à toi.

Np.

28*th*, 9 *a.m.* [28 *Sept.* 1811]

After a night inspection of the fort of Bath by torchlight, Napoleon reached Antwerp on September 30th, at one o'clock in the morning, and here he instructs Marie-Louise, who was in Brussels, to meet him.

Mon amie

I am reaching Antwerp by water. I write to you at once, you may set out at noon, so as to be here before dinner. I am in good health and shall be very glad to see you.

Nap.

ANTWERP 30 [*Sept.* 1811] 2 *a.m.*

The very same day the Imperial pair met at Antwerp. The bands struck up: *Où peut-on être mieux qu'au sein de sa famille?* While Antwerp is one of the ramparts of France, it is also one of her naval dockyards. On October 2nd, Napoleon and Marie-Louise presided over the launch of two warships, and there were a score of others on the stocks.

At Amsterdam, another visit was paid to a

dockyard on October 10th. When Marie-Louise arrived, in a gilded coach drawn by eight horses, the streets were gay with tricolour bunting, the windows decked with wreaths of flowers. Thence Napoleon proceeds to inspect the fortifications of the Helder, which he finds insufficiently provided with artillery. He had lunch on board the flag-ship of Vice-Admiral Dewinter, commanding the squadron of the Texel. And buttonholing him he observes: "Admiral, the Dutch are brave; they are good troops, steady under fire." Having been absent since October 15th from Amsterdam, where he had left the Empress and to which he returned the day after, he writes the following short notes to her:

Mon amie

I reached the Helder at 6 o'clock in the evening, and shall stop here all day. I shall therefore not reach Amsterdam to-day. I have had you told to go and see the village of Bru[i]ch; you can go to Haar-lem, as well. Take care of yourself and keep well. You do not question all the feelings of your f[aithful] husband.

NAP.

HELDER 16th, 3 a.m. [*Oct.* 1811]

The stars are shining. The day I am about to spend on board my squadron will be a fine one.

Mon amie

It is eight o'clock. I have been on the water all day. The weather was very fine. I had a good look at my squadron; I had it manœuvred. I visited the Island of Tesselle; and to-morrow, if it is fine, I shall remain another day to have my squadron manœuvred. I am never angry with you, because you are good and perfect and I love you. The little King is well. I am having you told to go and see the village of Bru[i]ch; go to Haarlem, as well. Adieu, mon amie. Keep well. You were quite right to take dis . . . wine . . . Tout à toi.

Nap.

9 p.m. 16, 8 (?) [16 *Oct.* 1811]

The impression left by the Imperial pair was excellent and the moral effect produced in the Netherlands by the Emperor's presence, enormous. No later than the year following, the Dutch gave proof of this by fighting on the side of the French during the Russian campaign.

III

THE RUSSIAN CAMPAIGN

"Like you, I am England's enemy", Napoleon had observed to Czar Alexander at the interview of Tilsit. The Czar was passionately attached to the Emperor, according to Caulaincourt, who was Ambassador to Russia. "I will part with him only if he compels me to do so", he declared. The Continental Blockade, which his subjects evaded, severed these bonds, as did, moreover, the veiled refusal of the hand of the Grand Duchess Anna, whom Napoleon at one time had in mind. And Russia gravitated into the orbit of England.

The passionate discussion between Napoleon and his Marshals, when the Russian campaign was contemplated, was a moving scene.

After vainly adducing every argument against going to war, Caulaincourt exclaimed: "Sire, my life belongs to you; do as you please with it on the battlefield. But in this case my convictions run contrary to yours; my conscience, my honour, belong to myself alone. I should be a coward, if in order to please Your Majesty, I were to betray the cause of France."

"What do you mean by that, sir?" retorted the Emperor, stepping angrily towards Caulaincourt.

"That this war is bound to result in grievous harm for the country; that all the Powers will rise against you. You are ruining yourself, Sire, and France is bound up with you."

The tension grew. The Czar Alexander was arming. Napoleon dispatched General the Comte de Narbonne-Lara as Ambassador Extraordinary to Russia. "Little Narbonne", for all his skill, met with no success. At Wilna, indeed, he dined at the Emperor's table, but the Czar dismissed him politely, by presenting him with his portrait, a formality the usual object of which was to mark the end of a mission. The Comte de Narbonne was advised, at the same time, that posthorses would be held ready for him at six p.m. There was no mistaking the significance of this message. On May 26th, Narbonne-Lara brought back an evasive reply to the Emperor. The Court was then at Dresden.

At Dresden, Napoleon was at the zenith of his power. Never had human greatness risen to such heights. He was the Agamemnon of the circle of Kings assembled there—the King of Kings. Marie-Louise "had the world at her feet", to quote the *Mémorial de Sainte-Hélène*. She lived between her father and her husband, between two Emperors, as an enamoured woman "jealously availing herself of the least of her husband's spare moments".

Doubly cruel for her, therefore, was Napoleon's departure on May 29th at half-past three in the morning. She made him promise to return promptly, in two months' time at most, which would appear to indicate that the Emperor was then contemplating a mere military demonstration. He kept control, indeed, of the affairs of the Empire, while taking command of the Army. Without pausing for the halts, he went through despatches and reports in his travelling carriage, which was fitted with a lamp for lighting him at night. The Major-General usually drove with him, while aides-de-camp and orderly officers rode at the carriage doors, ready to bear his despatches.

But whatever cares the day brought him—and there were many of an acute character—not a day was allowed to pass without a letter or a note addressed to the Empress leaving the Imperial quarters. And with what loving eagerness he awaited the reply!

"Let my mail never be delayed a single moment", he wrote in his instructions of March 16th, 1812, to the Postal Service. "The courier rode on without stopping to eat or drink or sleep. When the mail reached him, the Emperor had it slit open", if he had not the key of the valise.

"Usually", relates Baron Fain, "he never allowed a valise to be closed without dropping in a note to his wife. In such cases he did not dictate, but wrote himself. And not being used to this, it was a great business for him to write legibly. Give me a small sheet of nice paper', he would say to us; 'and a good pen! For, after all, cette bonne Louise must be able to read what I write'. And after writing, he would hand us the sheet folded in two and say to us: 'For the Empress'.

And when he was in a pleasant mood he would add: 'To the Lady of my Thoughts! To the Queen of my Heart!'"

On the very day of his departure, he sent off a message from Reichenbach in Upper Lausitz, the bearer of which was a Saxon officer.

RAINTENBACH 11 *a.m.*

Ma bonne Louise

I am stopping just a moment, for lunch. I am taking the advantage of the opportunity to write to you and urge you to be cheerful and not to worry. All my promises to you shall be kept; thus our absence from each other will be but a short one. You know how I love you; it is necessary for me to know you are in good health and easy in your mind. Adieu, douce amie. A thousand kisses.

N.

[REICHENBACH 29 *May* 1812]

From Glogau, twenty hours later, a second courier was sent on his way, with a request to the Empress to give him a token of gratitude: the presents handed over by the Grand Chamberlain, M. de Montesquiou, to the officers bearing the mails were to be proportionate to the more or less favourable character of the news:

GLOGAU 30*th*, 7 *a.m.*

Ma bonne Louise

I wrote to you yesterday. I arrived in good health at 2 o'clock in the morning. I came very fast. Just a little dust. I am leaving in time to be in Posen

this evening, and there I shall spend the day, to-
morrow the 31st. I hope you will have written to me
that you are in good health, that you are cheerful and
reasonable.   It is advisable, when I send you some
officers, that Montesquiou present them with diamond
rings, more or less handsome according to the news
they bring.   Your father will have taken his departure,
by this time, which must have still further increased
your loneliness.   Adio mio douce amore; a thousand
loving kisses.

N.

[30 *May* 1812]

And on the same day, May 30th, at 10 p.m.,
a third message left Posen, to be followed by
another the following day:

Mon amie

I have just arrived at Posen, rather incommoded by the dust; I am going to bed, but cannot do
so without writing you a few lines.   I have not yet
received your letters; I shall, to-morrow, I hope.
I trust, then, that you are in good health and that you
are reasonable.   Adieu, ma douce Louise.   I wish I
were with you; I shall, soon, I hope.   Tout à toi.

30 *May*, 10 *p.m.*   N.

31 *May*, 7 *p.m.*

I feel tired, having worked all day; I am going for
an hour's ride.   I have not yet heard from you, mon
amie; yet I am certain you have written to me, but I
travelled very fast.   I look forward to hearing that you
are in good health.   The Duc de Bassano, who will
arrive to-night, will bring me news of you.   Adieu,
my dear love; a tender kiss for Louise.

N.

POSEN

The Emperor had reached Poland. "A few one-storeyed wood and mud houses, standing in gardens fenced in with boards, here go by the name of a town", writes Castellane, a future Marshal. "After skirting the Warka, one comes to the plain in which lies the dismal town of Posen, one of the largest in Poland." On the occasion of Napoleon's arrival, on May 30th, a triumphal arch had been erected, bearing the inscription *Heroi invincibili*. And at night, on the façade of the Prefecture, where he had put up, the words *Grati Poloni Imperatori magno* shone forth in letters of fire. But since leaving Dresden, time hung heavily on his hands, on account of not seeing Marie-Louise "two or three times a day".

Mon amie

I received your three letters almost at the same time. I was beginning to think it a very long time to be two days without hearing from you. I am very sorry to hear you are feeling dejected and I am grateful to Princess Thérèse for taking you out. I am in very good health. I am leaving to-night, so as to be to-morrow morning at Thorn, where I shall be staying for several days. The Duc de Bassano has not arrived yet. Give my kind regards to your aunt and to the King and the Saxe family. It is quite right of you to think of me. You know I love you, and how vexed I am no longer to see you two or three times a day. But I am thinking it will be the case in 3 months' time. Adieu, mio dolce amore.

Tout à toi

N.

POSEN 1 *June, 6 p.m.*

At Thorn, Napoleon put up at the house of the Governor, General de Woyzinsky. The town was full of troops. Twenty-four officers and seventy-five men were quartered in one house only. Here are five infantry regiments of the Old Guard, of whom a review is to be held; here, too, is the main artillery park, which Napoleon does not fail to inspect in every detail, while his orderly officers are visiting the curious city, the birthplace of Copernicus, whose monument they admire in the Church of St. John. A host of twittering birds has taken advantage of the broken window-panes to invade the holy edifice. Here, General the Comte Louis de Narbonne-Lara brings to Napoleon letters from Marie-Louise:

Ma bonne Louise   THORN 3 *June*

Narbonne has brought me news of you, and he tells me you are very dejected. It is very wrong of you; you promised me to be brave and easy in your mind. You will be at Prague by this time, for you were to leave on the 4th. You will thus have the joy of being with your family, which will give you pleasure; I share in it. Give my kind regards to the Emperor. Tell the Empress I am at her feet, and how desirous I am to please her in all things. I shall be stopping here to-morrow to review my Guard, which is fully armed. Afterwards I shall run over to Danzig. I have good news from Paris. The King is in good health. Adieu, ma douce amour; love well him who loves you so well. Kind regards to your sisters. I should have wished very much to see Léopoldine and all your brothers and sisters whom I love on your account.

Tout à toi

N.

Ma bonne amie

I have received your letter of June 1st; you will see I had already been a longer time without hearing from you. I am leaving to-morrow for Danzick [Danzig]. You like Prague? I have ordered a courier to be sent to you at once. I think of you very often, I should like to see you, but I hope to do so before long. It is very hot, a good deal of dust. I was in the saddle this morning at 2 a.m., and was all the better for it. I have seen the Duc de Bassano, who spoke to me about you. Adieu, ma bonne Louise, do not worry. He told me you were taken with vomiting. Is this true? Kindest regards to all the family, as well as to your father and the Empress.

THORN 4*th*, 2 *p.m.* [4 *June* 1812]

Your
NAP.

Mon amie

I have received your letter of the 2nd. I was glad to hear you were in good health. Why do you get no sleep? It is most necessary for you. I expect the journey to Prague will do you good. It is very hot here, like in Italy; everything goes to extremes in this climate. Give my kind regards to your sisters and to your ladies-in-waiting. The little King is in good health; you have no doubt had news of him. I am leaving in an hour's time for Danzisc [Danzig]. Everything is quiet along the frontier. The Guards, whom I viewed yesterday, were looking splendid. Adieu, ma bonne Louise. I am as desirous as you are to meet you and I hope it will be soon. 3 months' absence and I am ever with you. A thousand kisses. You have not said anything more about your heart trouble. Please send me a line.

Your faithful
NAP.

THORN, *the 6th*, 1 *p.m.*

The departure from Thorn was homeric. It was to have taken place on June 6th, at four o'clock. It was only two o'clock when the Emperor, catching sight of Castellane, sent him to impart to the General Equerry his desire to leave at once.

"Impossible before three", was Castellane's reply.

"Have my saddle-horses brought round", Napoleon then cries to an orderly officer.

"Where is the Aide-de-Camp on duty?" he enquired as he mounted his horse. Not having expected so sudden a departure, General Lebrun was not to be found.

"Your horses?" the Emperor asks Castellane.

"Sire, they are on their way."

With an impatient growl the Emperor put spurs to his horse. And in a deafening uproar the whole retinue galloped off to join the Emperor. His carriage only came up with him a long way from Thorn.

* * *

Beyond Posen, the Emperor received letters from Marie-Louise. As reported by the *Gazette de France*, the Empress was moving about. In the outskirts of Dresden, she was being rowed about on the Elbe in a gondola, visiting the village of Tharandt, remarkable for its romantic setting and for a clump of elm trees known as the "Sacred Grove". Having left on June 4th for Bohemia, she was given a reception at Töplitz, a town on the frontier, which she entered by an archway adorned with wreaths of flowers and laurel leaves. And while on the walls were to be read the words: *A Louise, Impératrice des Français*, girls presented her with a basketful of flowers, and some miners, swinging their lanterns, punctuated their songs with cheers. At Prague, Marie-Louise passed under triumphal arches, escorted by squadrons of cavalry. Throughout the three weeks she stayed there, balls alternated with banquets, excursions with entertainments and illuminations.

Napoleon arrived unawares at Danzig on June 7th, at eight o'clock in the morning. No one expected him in the Free City. The next day, no later than 3 a.m., for it is daylight very early at this season of the year in this latitude, he proceeded to carry out an inspection of the fortifications, which lasted until twelve. At three o'clock in the afternoon, he received the Senate of the city, after which, until 8 p.m., he reviewed the troops. On the 9th, at daybreak, he visited the different points of the roads. Betweenwhiles he wrote to the Empress:

Mon amie

I arrived at Danzik [Danzig] very much incommoded by the dust. I am sending a special courier to Berlin, whence this letter will be forwarded to you, so that you may have news of me and not be uneasy. I shall stay here to-morrow, the 8th, as well as the 9th and perhaps the 10th. I hope you are quite well and enjoying yourself with your sisters; give them my kind regards. You have no idea of the sentiments I bear them for your sake. Mention me to your father, and tell him with what affection he has inspired me, and that he can rely on me. Tell the Empress I am at her feet. Give my kind regards to Madame Logisky (?).

Adio mio bene

Tout à toi

NAP.

The 7th, 10 *p.m.* [DANZIG 7 *June* 1812]

Ma bonne Louise

I have had no letters from you since that of the 4th, when you were leaving for Bohemia, but I hope to have some this evening and to hear you are pleased with your sisters and to be with your family. I am in the saddle from 2 o'clock in the morning, I get back at noon, sleep for 2 hours, and view the troops the rest of the day. My health is very good, the little King is well and is to be weaned shortly. I hope you have had news of him. I do so long to see you; in spite of my occupations and fatigue I feel there is something lacking—the sweet habit of seeing you several times in the course of the day. Adio mio bene. Keep well, be cheerful and contented, that is the way to please me.

Your faithful

NP.

The 9th, 6 *p.m.*

Ma bonne Louise

I have not heard from you since the 4th, that is for 7 days, but I hope to do so this evening, at Marienburg, where I shall put up for several [hours?]. I shall be at Koenigsberg to-morrow. My health is very good. I have written to you every day, so I suppose you will often have had letters from me. I want to hear you are enjoying yourself and are pleased with your sisters; give them my kind regards. All is very quiet along the frontiers. The weather has become rather rainy, and it has done good. See that you are contented and cheerful; it is the way to please me. Never doubt all the feelings I bear to il mio dolce amor. Give my kind regards to your father and to the Emperor. I expect to have news from Schwarzenberg to-morrow.

Ton affectionné

NP.

DANZIK, *the* 11*th*, 5 *p.m.*

From Marienburg, Napoleon sent off a very important letter concerning the bounties to be conferred both upon the members of the Empress's household, the dignitaries of the Court of Austria, and the Burgraves of Prague. The Empress's suite included the Grand Chamberlain, de Montesquiou; the Knight of Honour, Comte de Beauharnais; the First Equerry, Prince Aldobrandini Borghèse; the Chamberlains, Counts de Praslin, de Noailles, de Pange; the knights, Baron Dandelau, de Nesgrigny, de Lesseps; the Prefect of the Palace, Baron de Bausset; the Lady-in-waiting, Duchess de Montebello; the Ladies of the Palace, Duchesse de Bassano, Countesses de Brignole and de Beauvau. Prince Clary was at the head of the guard of honour appointed by the Emperor of Austria to attend Marie-Louise. And now let us read Napoleon's letter:

Ma bonne Louise MARIENBURG, *the* 12*th*, 7 *a.m.*

My anticipation was correct. I have received 4 letters from you, one when I was half way to this place, the 3 others this morning. I was surprised to

hear you had no letters from me yet. I sent 2 to my
Minister at Dresden, to be forwarded to you. You
must have greatly enjoyed seeing your sisters and
your uncles. Tell Prince Charles of all the esteem I
have for him. I presume you gave a present to Prince
Clary, at whose house you put up; it is the custom.
If not, do so when leaving Prague. Montesquiou
will have given the household all that was necessary.
You must be very generous and give a great deal in
every way. I had ordered presents to be procured
for the ladies-in-waiting of the Empress, the one for
Madame Lagisky (?) was to be worth 50,000 livres.
You will also give her one of the same value, so that
she may have 100,000 worth of diamonds, this
journey. You must not give gold snuff-boxes; that
is in bad taste. You must have rings, with your
monogram, worth 1,200, 2,000, 3,000 and 6,000
livres. Mention this to the High Chamberlain.
Give a great deal of money to all those who served
you formerly and to your old masters. I presume
Montesquiou has handed you your June allowance,
so that you may be able to spend a great deal. Jardin
has doubtless arrived to break in your mounts. Be
pleasant to your father and all your family. Talk to
the Emperor of all the feelings he has inspired me
with, tell the Empress I am at her feet. Make
enquiries as to whether there are any old customs
towards the Burgraves on the part of Sovereigns
passing through Prague. See, also, what you might
give, on leaving, to the city of Prague as a memento
of your visit. Adieu, mon amie; you know how I love
you. I want to know you are well and very cheerful.
Tell me you have got rid of that nasty cold. Never
allow anything ambiguous to be said in your presence
about France and politics.

Tout à toi

NAPOLEON

In the afternoon of June 12th, the Emperor arrived at Königsberg, where the Governor was a man devoted to him, the Dutch General Hogendorp. Here Napoleon remained for several days. On June 14th, in the interval between writing two letters to his wife, he reviewed the Polish Division under General Grandjean. He makes no mention of his accommodation in his letters. Now at the Hôtel de Paris, at which Castellane had put up, there was, according to the local custom, but one sheet on the beds, and as covering a feather bed which served indifferently for all travellers: it was "impossible to undress unless one slept in one's war-bag".

Over the old Prussian city, with its famous university, brooded the memory, the ghost of Kant, who had died eight years previously. And as though he had derived his inspiration from the author of the theory of transcendental idealism, which saw in "Eternal Peace" the goal of the historical development of mankind, the short week put in at Königsberg was for Napoleon a week of kindness. Upon the Empress, who rather archly taxed him with idleness, he lavished counsels of pity and generosity towards everybody, and above all towards the widows of Austrian military men and crippled soldiers. He was rejoiced to know she was loved:

Ma bonne et chère amie
      I have just received your letter of June 8th, in which you go into particulars about what you do with yourself. That gives me great pleasure. I like to know how you spend the day and what you see. I

shall be staying here to-morrow. You are mistaken in charging me with laziness. It seems to me I have sometimes written to you as much as twice a day. I am very grateful to your father for all he does to amuse you, he can do nothing that would please me better. I have none but good reports of the little King. I suppose you have news of him every day. I think of you very often, and though I work very hard, I very often wish to see you. I hope to do so in a few months' time. Give my kind regards to your sisters. You do not mention them. Remember me to them all. Are you satisfied with them? Tout à toi, dolce mio. N~p~.

KÖNIGSBERG 13 *June*, 7 *p.m.*

Ma bonne et chère Louise

I have received your letter of the 11th. I am thankful to see your cold has left you; take great care of yourself. Has Jardin arrived at last, so that you may go riding and accompany your father without fatigue? I am sorry to hear the Empress is ill. She does not take sufficient care of herself. The soul wears out the body. I greatly appreciate the good feelings of your uncles and sisters. Give my kind regards to Léopoldine. My health is perfect, I am leaving to-night for Vellau [Wehlau] where I shall hold some reviews. Be pleasant and kind to everybody, and especially very open-handed; give to all the ladies-in-waiting and Princesses and to all those who have served you. You may be god-mother to the child of your former lady-in-waiting and give her a handsome present in money. I am very glad to hear that every one loves you and to see you enjoy their affection. Be careful to give to needy wives and widows of Austrian army men, as well as to any broken soldiers who may be in want.

Adio, mio bene. Tout à toi. Pray do not forget to remember me to your father and to the Empress. N.

KÖNIGSBERG, *the* 16*th*, 3 *p.m.*

IV

THE GRANDE ARMÉE

THE Grand Army was a babel of races and
languages. Jerome Bonaparte, King of Westphalia, commanded an army made up of Poles,
Westphalians and Saxons; Schwarzenberg had
Austrians under him; Oudinot, Duc de Reggio,
French, Swiss and Croat troops; a regiment of
Corsican Tirailleurs, and Roman, Piedmontese
and Florentine conscripts were brigaded with
a Dutch regiment; Marshal Ney's Corps was
made up of one Wurtemberg and two French
divisions. . . . And Castellane, who rubbed
shoulders with all these troops, thanks to the
facilities afforded to an officer in the Emperor's
personal service, must doubtless have omitted
some of them, for there was also a Portuguese
contingent.

At Wehlau, the Emperor reviewed the Cuiras-
sier Division. At Insterburg, on June 15th, it
was the turn of Oudinot's Corps, of two brigades
of light cavalry, and Kleat's Prussian Brigade.
The following day, at Gumbinnen, the Emperor
held a review of the First Army Corps. And in
the midst of these military cares, he writes to
Marie-Louise:

Ma bonne Louise

A few lines only. Méneval has lain sick at Danzig for the last 6 days, and is feverish. I am in very good health. I am all day long with the troops, reviewing and commanding them. I am leaving this afternoon for Gunbinen where I shall be in three hours' time. Adieu, mon amie. I think of you. I have not heard from you to-day, or yesterday, but I hope to do so to-morrow. Tout à toi. Adio mio. Many kind regards to your family.

ISTENBURG [INSTERBURG], *the* 18*th*, *noon*.

Napoleon's secretary, Baron Méneval, was one of the earliest friends of the Bonaparte family. And he was destined to play the part of confidant in the matrimonial drama that marked the end of Napoleon's career.

Isabey, to whon the Emperor presently refers, was likewise an old-time friend and the author of the portrait of Bonaparte at Malmaison, of the charming portraits of Marie-Louise with a garland of roses, and of the roi de Rome in his cradle; he was also the painter of official ceremonies. The Empress had even taken him to give her lessons in drawing on condition the master did not touch up the drawings of the pupil. Isabey had just returned from Vienna, where he had painted the portraits of the Austrian Imperial Family.

Ma bonne Louise

I have received your letter of June 14th. I am glad to hear you are well and that Jardin has arrived; riding will do you good. I am informed by people in Paris that Isabei has left for Prague. It will be all right for you to write a few lines to Méneval once. Have your thanks conveyed to King Louis— you must never call him the King of Holland—for any messages he sends you, and tell him at the same time that he should return to France; that in spite of all his faults I cannot forget that I brought him up like a son. My health is very good. Deliver pleasant assurances to the Empress from me and many compliments to your father, whom I love for the care he bestows on you and the love he bears you. The weather is rather hot to-day. I am leaving to-morrow to review an Army Corps, the day after to-morrow, the Austrian Corps which arrived at Lublin on the 22nd. Adieu, me chère Louise, I am very desirous of seeing you and I kiss your beautiful lips. Tout à toi.

NAP.

GUMBINEN, *the* 20*th*, 5 *p.m.*

An expression of filial love for the Emperor, kind regards to the Empress of Austria: observe the nuance. "Papa François", easy-going to the point of doing his own marketing, had been won over by his son-in-law and has signed the Treaty of Alliance of March 12th. Marie-Louise-Béatrice d'Este, Marie-Louise's young step-mother, nurses all manner of grievances against Napoleon: the misfortunes of her family, de-throned in Italy; humiliation on the score of Austria's defeats; humiliation caused by the munificence of Marie-Louise, who can afford to give presents to her stepmother. Napoleon failed to win her over at Dresden by his genteel bearing, though he went so far as to escort the sedan-chair in which she used to have herself carried about. And with Metternich's connivance, the betrayal was secretly framed: the Czar is given the assurance that Austria's auxiliary troops will not exceed the figure of twenty-six thousand men.

Napoleon's letter thus lays down for his young wife a whole line of conduct. She is not to exasperate the dethroned King of Holland. While Louis Bonaparte, in a moment of anger, had published a libel against his brother, the latter had treated him, in his youth, like a son. Méneval, who had known Louis in Paris, under the Directory, said of the future King that this friend of belles-lettres was good and upright at heart, to the point of adopting for his motto: "*Fais ce que dois, advienne que pourra*".

The next few letters of the Emperor's are brimful of love and show a constant desire to please his wife's family. Nor was this anxiety devoid of an underlying political motive. The assistance of Austria against Russia was of vital interest for him.

Ma bonne amie
      I have received your letter of the 13th. I am very sorry to hear your health is weak and that you are grieving. I am very grateful indeed to your father for trying to amuse you. You do not refer to

NAPOLEON'S DREAM

NAPOLEON'S HANDWRITING

the rest of your uncles. Do they not intend to come and see you? My health is very good. I am often in the saddle; it does me good. I am given favourable news of the King. He is growing, he has learned to walk and he is in good health. I am sorry to hear that what I hoped has not materialized; well, it must be put off till next autumn. I hope to hear from you to-morrow. Adieu, mon bien, be cheerful [and] satisfied for the sake of your health. Tout à toi.

NP.

GUMBINEN 19 *June*

I am leaving in an hour's time, ma bonne Louise, [for] Wilcoviki [Wilkowiszki] to view some troops. [I have received] your letter of the 15th, in which you speak to me of the da [. . .]. Tell[1] him that I have appointed his brother officier [dans la] Légion d' honneur. My health is very [good]. You make no mention of your uncle Rudolf[?] Keep on writing to Prague. I have no objection to conferring a decoration upon your uncle's Chamberlain. Let me have his name and country and tell me whether he intends to serve abroad. The King is in very good health, so I am informed. You know how I love you. I should so like to have you with me; it is a sweet habit I have acquired. I hope to revert to that habit in a few months' time. Adieu, mon amie; be satisfied [and] good, and love one who loves you so well.

NAP.

GUMBINEN 21 *June*

Ma bonne Louise

I am here. I am leaving in an hour's time. The heat is excessive. We are in the dog days. My health is good. I shall receive a letter from you this

[1] A tear in the paper.

afternoon. I do beg you to take care of yourself and to keep well, you know the interest I take in you. I hope to find you in good health three months hence. The little King is in the very best of health, I am told. Let me know when you propose to leave; be sure you travel by night, for the dust [and] heat are very fatiguing and might affect your health, but if you travel at night, by easy stages, you will bear the journey well. Adieu, ma bonne amie. Sincere feelings of love.

NAP.

WICOWISKI [WILKOWISZKI] 22 *June*

Wilkowiszki! A poor collection of cottages, swarming at the moment with troops, overrun by seventy-five thousand men under Davout. To these the Emperor issues an ardent proclamation: "Soldiers, the second Polish War has started. The first was brought to an end at Friedland and at Tilsit; at Tilsit, Russia swore everlasting alliance with France and war with England. To-day she breaks her plighted word. . . . She confronts us with dishonour or war. There can be no doubt about our choice. Forward!"

A further proclamation followed: "Soldiers, you have fought with me in three parts of the world. Whithersoever I led you, victory was your slogan. The French Eagles will for the second time be raised on high beyond the Oder and the Vistula. . . . After this last struggle, which will bring you the last laurel-leaves of your victory, I shall conclude a peace worthy of my people and of myself."

After taking supper at two o'clock in the

morning in the garden of the Curé of Skrawden, Napoleon, in the uniform of a Polish Lancer, repaired to the outposts.

In echelon, on the west bank of the Niemen, were arrayed the several Army Corps of Schwarzenberg, abutting on Galicia, of King Jerome of Westphalia, and Prince Eugène de Beauharnais. In the centre, Napoleon had Murat, Ney, Oudinot, Lefebvre and Bessières with the Guard; on the left wing, at Tilsit, were Macdonald and the Prussians.

This meant a front of close upon half a million men.

By an indiscreet report in the German *Gazette de Saint-Pétersbourg*, Napoleon had been apprised of the various armies opposing him: Barclay de Tolly was posted behind the Niemen; Tormassof, behind the Bug; Bagration, in the neck between the two rivers; Tchitchagoff, in Moldavia. In all, according to Colonel Buturlin, 250,000 men.

Flowing in a valley shaded by forests of limes and oak trees, between lofty rocks crowned by slumbering burgs, the Niemen marked the frontier between Poland and Russia. On June 24th, at sunrise, the left bank afforded an imposing spectacle. On the loftiest height was set up the Emperor's tent; all around the low hills were thronged with men in brilliant uniforms. By three bridges thrown over the river by Eblé, this mass streamed across to the right bank. In two days, 300,000 men thus crossed over. *"Marlborough s'en va-t-en guerre"*, hummed Napoleon.

But who would be put in mind of the seriousness of such things by the following letter, in which the Sorbonne takes up as much space as the war:

Mon amie

        I crossed the Niemen on the 24th, at two o'clock in the morning. I crossed the Viliya in the afternoon. I am master of Kovno. No affair afterwards. All at my entry. My health is good, but the heat is overpowering. I have just received your letter of the 18th: I am very grateful indeed to the Emperor for all his marks of affection towards you and for the care he takes of you. Remember me to him. You can present the University with a collection of books and engravings. This will please it vastly and will cost you nothing. I have plenty of them. Adieu, mon amie. Tout à toi.

NAP.

KOVNO, *morning of the 25th*

The die was cast. Between the emperors who had mutually defied each other like two braggarts—to quote the *Memorial de Sainte-Hélène*—war was declared. An unfortunate omen for the superstitious: as he was about to cross the Niemen, like Cæsar crossing the Rubicon, Napoleon was thrown from his horse: a hare starting up between its legs had caused his mount to shy and unseat the Emperor.

The letter written on the day following announced the despatch of the first Bulletin de la Grande Armée.

KOVNO 26 *June*

Mon amie

Méneval is sending you the first Army orders. I am leaving to-night. I shall be at Vilna the day after to-morrow. My affairs are going well, my health is good and I think of you, and I am glad to read in your letters how your father takes care of you; it is a source of great pleasure to me. Thank him on my behalf. I approve of the presents you intend to confer upon Prague. I consider it quite right. Be cheerful. We shall meet at the time I promised you we should. Tout à toi.

Ton

NAP.

"My affairs are going very well." Are they, though? A blow in the air. No coming to grips. The Russians have vanished. On June 28th, at dawn, a party of Hussars bring in an officer with a flag of truce, Balachof, the Czar's aide-de-camp, with his trumpeter: "Let the Grande Armée cross back over the Niemen", suggests Alexander, "and war will be avoided". A blind, thinks Napoleon. And his reply is: "No". "The enemy has been properly thwarted", he writes to the Empress.

Ma bonne amie

I am at Vilna, very busy; my affairs are going very well indeed, the enemy has been properly thwarted, I am in the best of health, I think of you. I know you are very satisfied with the attentions of your father, who takes great care of you; thank him on my behalf; give my kind regards to all; I sympathize with the Empress in her illness. The little King is in very good health. Vilna is a very fine city of 40,000 souls. I have my quarters in a rather fine mansion, where the Emperor Alexander was living a few days ago, very far from thinking at the time that I was so soon to enter here. Adieu, mon amie. Tout à toi.

NAP.

VILNA 30 *June*, 1 *p.m.*

At Vilna, the Emperor has gained possession of the Czar's Palace, but not of the huge supplies of the Russian Army, of which nothing remains but smoking ruins. On entering the town, with its dark winding streets, he was sadly disappointed. No decorations. Silence everywhere. Torrential rain alternates with scorching heat. On the very day when the Emperor entered Vilna, Oudinot had a brush with Wittgenstein at Wilkomir.

The advance of the French Army cut the Russian forces in two. Attacked by Davout on the road to Moghileff, Bagration would have been compelled to surrender, had it not been for the incapacity of King Jerome, who allowed him to escape. It was now impossible, however, for him to take the French in the rear as he had been instructed to do.

At his headquarters in Vilna, Napoleon set up a provisional Government for Lithuania. On the right bank of the Viliya, he established an intrenched camp and had a citadel built on the hill where stood the old Palace of the Jagellons. And the bulletins of the Grande Armée blazon forth to the world the "transports of joy and gratitude caused by the precious gift of liberty bestowed upon four million men".

VILNA I *July*

Mon amie

I have received your letter. The ladies-in-waiting you suggest for service during the next three months appear to me to be suitable. Choose whom you please among the office for your service. Am remaining 3 days at Würzburg (?) Provided you are at Saint Cloud some time in July, it will be sufficient. Make a present to your former Grand Master. I will grant the pension you ask for Madame Lazansky's (?) protégée. The weather is very rainy, the storms in this country are frightful, it has been raining in torrents for the last three days. My affairs are going well. My health is good. Adieu, mon amie, you know how deeply I love you.

NAP.

Amid the cares of a terrific campaign, in which he has close upon half a million men under his orders, Napoleon finds time to attend to the needs of the Empress's protégées, including her former governess. Out of an allowance of 25,000 francs granted to her by Napoleon, Countess Lazansky has certain people to provide for. As for the former Grand Master, Count Edling, whose appetite has been whetted by the success of his claims, the Emperor has gone so far as to write a letter recommending him to Andréossy, the head of a section of the Council of State.

Ma bonne amie

     I have just received your letter of June 22nd, in which I read that your father continues taking care of you, and that riding agrees with you. We are having great heat here, and very heavy rain to-day, which interferes with us and to our harm. My affairs are going well, my health is good and I often think of you. Adieu mio ben.

NAP.

    WILNA 2 *July* 1812

"Riding will do you good." The year before, the Emperor, in silk stockings and shoes with buckles on them, had been for a ride with her and taken a canter by her side.

Mon amie

     It grieved you very deeply to leave your father, who has been so kind for you. I share in your sorrow. You are just now (?) with the excellent Grand Duke of Wurtemberg; you can travel by easy stages. You will be welcomed in France. People would be aggrieved were you to come incognito. Stop a day or two at Mayence. You may spend a day at Compiègne and you will arrive early at Saint Cloud. The Pope is at Fontainebleau. Have enquiries made of him at your arrival at Saint Cloud, how his health is, and whether he is comfortable; you can write him a short note, without any show of affectation, however. Adieu, mon amie. The weather is sultry. My affairs are going well. Tout à toi.

NAP.

    VILNA 8 *July*

72

Pope Pius VII was at Fontainebleau. "Have enquiries made of him." And in writing to His Holiness Marie-Louise forgets to sign her letter in the customary form, of which Secretary Méneval will have to send her a copy: "Votre très chère fille." This momentous event, a reminder of the time when the Popes had taken up their abode at Avignon, and of the Great Schism, takes but three lines to record. It marks the goal of the Imperial policy. Pius VII, who had come to Paris for the purpose of crowning the Emperor, had witnessed the military occupation of Rome in 1809, for having refused to expel enemy subjects from the Papal States, and for having proclaimed that as the Vicar of Christ he prescribed the duty of peace towards all men without distinction. The excommunication he launched was immediately followed in July, 1809, by his arrest. And it was from Savona, where he was too much within gunshot and at the mercy of the British cruisers, that the Pope came and took up his abode at Fontainebleau. This fact accounts for the somewhat free and easy terms of the Imperial missive: "You can write him a short note, without any show of affectation." The Emperor has left behind him, without having been able to bring it about by assembling the Council of 1811, the allaying of men's consciences.

Mon amie
        I have received no letters from you to-day. I hope to see you at Würzburg. You will soon be seeing the little King, who will know you before he knows

me; you will find him much grown after three months' absence. My affairs are going well, my health is good, and I ask you tell the Queen of Spain how I sympathize with her in her illness. I hope she will soon have recovered. Adio mio ben; keep in good health. Never have any doubts.

NAP.

VILNA 12 *July*

Ma bonne amie

I have just received your letter from Egre, in which I read that you are about to take leave of your father, and that you have received the first bulletin. Make the presents you suggest. I approve of them. My affairs are going well; my health is good. We have storms and bursts of heat, alternately. The crops here will be first-rate. I envy you the happiness it will give you to kiss the little King; kiss him for me. He will have grown by this time. Let me know if he is beginning to talk. Adio mio ben; you know how I love you.

Tout à toi
N.

VILNA 14 *July* [1812]

Ma bonne amie

I have received no letters from you for many days. I hope, however, that you [are] in good health. You have arrived in France. My health is very good. Kiss the little King for me. Love me and never doubt my sentiments. My affairs are going well. Adieu. Tout à toi.

VILNA, *the* 16*th*, 10 *p.m.*

Napoleon's thoughts follow the Empress on her return journey. She had taken leave of her father at Egra on July 6th. On the 7th she was at Würzburg, where her uncle, the Grand Duke Ferdinand, affords her, together with the pleasure of excursions in the country, the hearing of concerts in which he displays his talent as "precentor". Thence, she proceeds to Mayence where, as recommended by her husband, she remains but one day, to be treated, on the next day, July 16th, to the most lavish hospitality by his Chamberlain, Count de Pange.

She is sad: "God grant I may soon meet the Emperor", she writes to her father; "for this separation weighs much too heavily upon me."

And the almost uninterrupted succession of her letters, of which we have, unfortunately, but the dates, revealed by the Emperor's notes, bears witness to her attachment: July 6th, 8th, 10th from Würzburg, 12th, 15th from Mayence, 18th from Châlons, 19th from Compiègne, 19th, 20th, 22nd, 23rd, 24th, 28th from Saint-Cloud or from Paris.

On August 15th, the Emperor's patron saint's day, she has to take his place at the official receptions of the authorities and Ambassadors, as stated in the following note, written from the Convent of Gloubokoye, where he attends Mass:

Mon amie
      I am staying here in a Carmelite Convent, in lonely country, but flourishing. As you can see, I am 60 leagues from Vilna, further away from you.

I hope that you have arrived at Saint Cloud. Kiss your little son for me twice; reports say he is charming.

Express my satisfaction to Madame Montesquiou for her care. I presume that you have made her come to Saint Cloud in order to have her with you. I think it would be seemly for you to go to Paris on my birthday, doing as I should do in order to attend the public concert; you can also receive the authorities and the Ambassadors and hold a great Court and a fine spectacle. Adieu, mio dolce amore. Keep well. Go and see the Queen of Spain every 3 days as long as she is indisposed. Give her many kind messages from me. Comfort her little daughter.

NAP.

GLOUBOKOS, *the* 18*th*, 1 *p.m.*

Madame Montesquiou, on her appointment as "Governess to the Imperial Children"—the plural being used although there was, as yet, but one— has sworn "obedience to the Constitutions and fealty to the Emperor". "I promise", she has declared, "to serve with diligence and devotion, in all the duties of the function entrusted to me by His Majesty, the children it may please His Majesty to entrust to my care."

The Countess of Montesquiou, née Le Tellier de Louvois, was a devout woman of unbending character: "Madam", said the Emperor, "I entrust to you the destinies of France. Make my son a good Frenchman and a good Christian." And seeing a smile on the lips of some of the courtiers, he added: "The one cannot go without the other." During the absence of his father and mother, it was she who took their place with the

King of Rome. And Marie-Louise, on her return, finds in her son a delightful child, a "charming little monkey", who will thenceforth be referred to in every one of the Emperor's letters: "Tell me if you were much struck with him, if he is beginning to talk, if he has begun to walk . . ."

Ma bonne et chère amie

 I wrote to you yesterday. I have no news from you. My health is good. I suppose you are at Saint Cloud. I pray you to be cheerful and to keep in good health. My affairs here are progressing very well. I am staying in a Carmelite Convent. I am going to Mass, it is Sunday.

                NAP.

 GLOUBOKOS, *the* 19*th of July, noon*

Ma bonne amie

 I have just received your letter of the 8th of July from which I see that you must have gone to Saint Cloud to-day the 19th. Kiss the little King twice for me. Tell me whether he has impressed you much, whether he is beginning to talk, whether he is walking, and finally, if you are satisfied with his progress. My health is very good. I could not wish for more in this respect, and I feel better than in Paris; my affairs are going well. The only thing that I miss is my good Louise, but I am glad to know that she is with my son. The Parisians must have been glad to see you. Adieu, mon amie. Give many messages to your ladies and to the Grand Duchess. I love you always. Tout à toi.

                NAP.

 GLOUBOKOS, *the* 19*th,* 4 *p.m.*

Ma bonne Louise

I have just received your letter of the 10th from Wurzburg. You were right to rejoice at the thought of seeing the little King. By this time you will have written to me how you found him and what impression he has made on you. My health is very good, my affairs are going well. I beg you to send suitable greetings from me to the Grand Duke when you write to him as well as to your father. I hope that you will have been satisfied with Paris and with France and that you will have seen it with pleasure. Adieu, mio bene. Tout à toi.

They will look for the book which you have asked for, and it will be sent to you.

Nap.

GLOUBOKOS 21 *July*

The Grand Duke of Würzburg, Marie-Louise's uncle, is the former Duke of Tuscany, Ferdinand. Transferred by the wand of the Imperial enchanter from Florence to Salzburg, and thence to Würzburg, he just missed being raised to the throne of Austria in 1809. A familiar acquaintance of Napoleon's since the days when he was but General Bonaparte, the wandering Prince now coveted Poland in exchange for his Grand Duchy.

Mon amie

I have received your letter of the 12th of July, from which I see that you have had a little fever. You do not take sufficient care of yourself. I thank you for the good news which you give me of the little

King.   Everyone says that he is very strong and very greedy.   By this time you will have kissed him, which will have done you much good.   Kiss him for me. Adieu, ma douce amie.   Love me always.   Tout à toi.   Ton
                                                        NAP.

GLOUBOKOE 22 *July*

Yes, Marie-Louise is feverish, of nights, at least every third day.   The cause of this? Anxiety, the absence of Napoleon.   "Try and be reasonable and easy in your mind, and we will cure you", say the physicians.

"We are still advancing."   There is no mention of the fight at Ostrovno, of which Murat and Eugène de Beauharnais have been the heroes, or of others either.   Read the tenth bulletin of the Grand Army.   "The enemy deployed fifteen thousand horse and sixty thousand foot . . ." The Emperor was posted on a height close by the two hundred "voltigeurs" (light infantrymen) who, alone in the plain, had attacked the right of the enemy cavalry.   Struck with their stalwart appearance, he sent to enquire to what corps they belonged.   "To the ninth Corps", was the reply, "and three-quarters of us are born Parisians." "They all deserve the cross", said the Emperor.

In the evening of July 27th, Napoleon was in camp opposite Vitebsk, which he entered the next day.

KAMEN 24 *July, Noon*

I will not let 2 days pass without writing to you, mon amie.   We are having much rain, the weather is hot, we keep on marching.   I have not received a courier since yesterday, I have marched too far. I am holding a Parade this evening. I trust that you are now in Paris and in good health. Kiss my son. Adieu, mio bene. Tout à toi.

NAP.

Mon amie

My health is very good. My affairs are going well. I love you, you know it. I rejoice to know that you are with your son. I have crossed the Dwina here, I am marching on Vitpsk, one of the great cities of this country. The harvest is magnificent and looks wonderful. Tout à toi.

NAP.

BECHENKOVISKI, *the* 25*th*, 2 *p.m.*

Mon amie

I have received your letter of the 15th from Mayence. I see with pleasure that you are in France. I am looking forward to news of the little King; you must have found him much grown. I hear that he eats enough for four and that he is very greedy. My health is fairly good. My affairs are going well. Adieu, mon amie. Tout à toi.

NAP.

BECHENCHOVITZI [BESCHENKOWITSCHI] 26 *July*

VITEBSK, 28*th*, 2 *p.m.*

I send you a line lest you should be anxious. My affairs are going well. My health is good, the heat is great. I love you much. Kiss my son. Adieu, mon amie.

NAP.

Many letters are dated from Vitebsk, for the Emperor remained there for several days. There being no hope left of breaking up Barclay's force separately, he has gone into cantonments, on the Dwina, with his army reinforced by the Army Corps of Davout, Poniatowski and the West-phalians, whom King Jerome, the strategist, has left. He orders outworks to be thrown up to cover the town, has forts built as though the army was to go into winter quarters there, but soon he loses patience and in spite of the objections of Duroc, Caulaincourt and Narbonne, decides upon a further advance. Of the fourteen letters addressed to Marie-Louise from Vitebsk only one gives an inkling of the plan which looms ahead: "We are now but 100 leagues from Moscow."

Mon amie

The last letter I have received from you was from the Château de Compiègne. You must have arrived early at Saint Cloud, and you will have had the pleasure of seeing your son walk to meet you. Kiss him for me. The weather is very warm. My health is good. My affairs are going well. You know how much I love you. Write to me from Paris everything that comes to your knowledge and what is being said. Adieu, mon amie. Keep well. Tout à toi.

Nap.

VITEPS[K] 30 *July*

Mon amie

I have just received your letter from Chalons dated the 18th of July at 4 o'clock in the morning. I see with pleasure that you are in very good health. You must have arrived at Saint Cloud by now. The little King will begin to know you, he will be a companion for you. Keep well, and be cheerful. My affairs are going well, but the heat is excessive; yesterday we had 26 degrees of heat. Adieu, mon amie, tout à toi.

NAP.

VITEPSK 1 *Aug.*

Ma bonne amie

I have just received your letter of the 19th. It seems that the little King was in a bad temper. I am glad that he called Papa for help. You were quite right to retain the Chamberlains and Equerries who suit you. Here we are having unbearable heat, 27 degrees. This is as hot as in the South. My health is good. My affairs are going well. I love you and I hope to receive to-morrow news and details about your son.

NAP.

VITEPSK 2 *Aug.*

Mon amie

I have just received your letter of the 20th of July. The page whom you have sent me will not arrive before another 8 days, I am therefore annoyed that you should have sent the details about the little King by him. Madame Montesquiou pretends that he recognized you; this seems to me somewhat exaggerated. Adieu, mon amie, I love you.

NAP.

Mon amie

I have just received your letter of the 22nd of July. I have given orders that they should continue to give you for your privy purse 20,000 a month until my return. I hear with pleasure that you are well. The heat here is very great. My health is good. My affairs are going well. Adieu, mon amie. Tout à toi. Ton

NAP.

VITEPSK 5 *Aug.*

Ma bonne et chère Louise

I have received your letter of the 23rd of July in which you give me good news of the little King. I am pleased to hear that your health is good. The heat here is much greater than in Vienna, it wearies me. My affairs are going well. I am very well. I have promised you some fine feathers for your Saint's Day for which I send you my good wishes. Adieu, ma bonne amie, Ton

NAP.

6 *Aug.* 1812

Mon amie

I have just received your letter of the 24th in which you inform me of the little King's good health. The heat here is greater than in Paris, we are suffocating. My affairs are going well, I am very well. Here we are only 100 leagues from Moscow. Believe in my sincere love.

NAP.

VITEPSK 7 *Aug.*

Mon amie

I have received your letter of the 25th of July. I see with pleasure that the heat in Paris is not excessive as it is here. The little King must amuse you a great deal if he is beginning to talk and to feel. I hear that he is a little rascal, very greedy and very noisy. My health is very good. The harvest is to be got in here, it will only begin in 8 or 15 days. Keep well. I know that you are used to keeping your time fully occupied; this is a very valuable and very necessary thing, it is one of your great qualities. Adieu, mio bene. Tout à toi.

NAP.

VITEPSK 8 *Aug.*

Mon amie

My first page Centurion has just arrived, he has just handed me your letter and given me news of you which pleases me. Your letter to the Pope is good but you must end it with the formula "Votre très chère fille," etiquette requires it. I am asking Méneval to send you a draft of it. Have a message sent to Madame Beauvau (?) that I share her sorrow. You can receive people in audience during my absence but be careful that it is proper and only persons who deserve it. As regards the French women you can send me the list in advance, as regards foreign women you can receive them provided they conform to custom. I cannot remember what it is you ask me concerning the 120,000 livres for the present. If it is the present which you have made to your family it seems to me that I had already given orders about it. I do not understand either about the Dutch lace, however you will find herewith orders which will enable you to arrange all this. I rely on you. Adieu, mon amie; kiss the little King and never doubt your faithful

NAP.

VITEPSK 9 *Aug.*

Mon amie

You can give the entrée to the mother of the Princess of Neufchâtel; invite her to dinner and show her some politeness. She is a worthy person, a sister of the King of Bavaria and the Princess of Saxony. My health is very good, we are having much rain. My affairs are going well. I beg you to look after yourself well. Kiss the little King for me; he will already be able to speak when I return. Adieu, mon amie, tout à toi.

NAP.

VITEPSK 10 *Aug.*

Mon amie

I have just received your letter of the 28th of July. I hear it is also very hot in Paris; the Saint Cloud air must be good for you and the little King. Kiss him for me, take many walks and be happy. My health is good, my affairs are going well. I kiss you. Ton

NAP.

VITEPSK 11 *Aug.*

Ma bonne Louise

I cannot understand how you can have been 2 days without receiving any letters of mine; perhaps no courier has reached you, for I write to you every day. You might increase the number of persons, women and men, to whom you give the entrée. You have not put enough on [the list] in order to have a few people every day. Add La Valette, his wife and a dozen others. I do not agree with you. Women are lighter and less serious than we are. I am pleased with the good news you give me of my son. Adieu, mon amie; my health is very good.

NAP.

The 11*th*, 11 *p.m.*

Mon amie

I have just received your letter of the 18th in which I see that your health is good, mine is excellent. It has been raining for 3 days. I should like to be with you for your Saint's Day[1] as last year and to tell you how much I love you. Do have no doubt about it, have you? Adieu, mon amie. Tout à toi.

The 12*th*, 10 *p.m.*

NAP.

[1] *i.e.* the day of St. Louis, August 25th.

85

The advance on Moscow was decided upon in the morning of July 29th, at the Palace of the Prince of Wurtemberg, Governor of White Russia, after a lengthy conference with Poniatowski, Lefebvre-Desnouettes and Berthier. In one of the letters printed above, there is a mention of Berthier or at least of his wife. Major-General Berthier, Prince de Neuchâtel, had married a Bavarian Princess, Elisabeth Marie, niece to the King of Bavaria.

The Imperial letter, dated from Krasnoie, makes no mention of the fight that had occurred there the day before. Following upon a clever manœuvre that brought the French troops to the rear of Bagration's army, Murat's cavalry had boldly broken up the Noworovski Division, posted by Bagration in the direction of Krasnoie, as a flank guard. Noworovski had about a thousand killed and a great many wounded.

Mon amie

I am writing in my tent, for I have started my advance on Smolensk. I have received your letter of the 19th. My health is very good, the details you give me regarding the Viceroy are very interesting. It is a lucky thing to see you beside him.

Adieu mon amie. Tout à toi.

Your faithful

KRASNOI 15 *Aug.* NAP.

A real battle was at last begun under the walls of Smolensk. The Emperor's intention was to turn the left of the Russian armies so as to cut them off from Moscow and drive them back towards the Lower Dwina. Smolensk, a smiling town lying amphitheatre-wise on both banks of the Dnieper, was surrounded with a big brick wall reinforced by turrets. Deep ravines covered it. Rafewski and Poskiowicz's resistance gave Doctorof time to hasten up. Ney, who led the attack, was supported by Davout and Poniatowski. Barclay sent reinforcements to his troops, but in the night of August 17th–18th, he decided to evacuate the town, leaving it all aflame. In the early morning, Napoleon effected his entry.

SOMOLENSK 18 *Aug.*

Mon amie

I am in Somolensk since this morning. I captured this town from the Russians after having killed 3,000 of them and wounded or taken prisoner more than three times that number. My health is very good, the heat excessive. My affairs are going well. Schwarzenberg has defeated the Russians 200 leagues from here.

NAP.

Mon amie

I have just received your letter of the 6th of August, it is cold in Paris, and here the heat is frightful. My affairs are going well, my health is good; here I have been in camp and in action (?) every day. Adieu, mon amie; kiss my son, you must find him grown and intelligent, my Louise. Adio ben mio.

NAP.

SMOLENSK 20 *Aug.*

Smolensk was an important base, and a refuge to fall back upon. Here, Napoleon appointed as Governor a first-rate technician, who had published at Glogau, in 1807, his famous book, the *Principes fondamentaux de l'Art de la Guerre*, much admired by the Czar. And Jomini was loth to take an active part in the campaign against the forces of Alexander, whose aide-de-camp he had come near being.

The delicate thought had occurred to Marie-Louise of sending the Emperor the portrait of his son as a birthday present. And she had instructed a Privy Councillor, Débonnaire de Cif, who was taking the Ministers' reports to the Emperor, to hand to him at the same time the miniature she had had painted, not by Isabey, but by Mlle. Aimée Thibault. The King of Rome was depicted astride a sheep. The miniature was kept by the Emperor to his dying day.

Mon amie

I have received a beautiful picture of the little King which Isabey sent me on Thursday (?) by my Commissioner. I found it a good likeness and very beautiful. Kiss him for me twice. My health is very good, my affairs are going well, the heat is excessive. Adio mio ben. Keep well and do not doubt your

NAP.

SMOLENSK 22 *Aug.*

Following upon the portrait of the son, two letters from the mother reached Smolensk in close succession.

SMOLENSK

(17th August, 1812—10 p.m.)

From a drawing by Fabre de Faure

THE NEW PROMISE OF HAPPINESS
(The King of Rome.)

Mon amie

I have just received your letter of the 10th of August. I am grieved to see that you have been 3 days without receiving any of my letters. I am pleased with the news which you give me of the little King and of your health. I am glad that you are satisfied with the Parisians. Adieu, mon amie. Tout à toi.

NAP.

SOMOLENSK 23 *Aug.*

Mon amie

I have just received your letter of the 11th of August. It seems that it is not so hot in Paris as it is here; to-day we have a temperature of 26 degrees, this weather has been going on for a month. It appears from all that you tell me that the little King is decidedly greedy. My health is very good, my affairs are going well. Adieu, mon amie, tout à toi.

SMOLENSK 24 *Aug.*

NAP.

Ma bonne amie

I travelled all day yesterday. I have moved my Headquarters forward to this place, the enemy has not waited for me, my vanguard is 40 leagues from Moscow. The heat is extreme, my health very good, my affairs are going well. I send you my best wishes for a happy Saint's Day. I envy the happiness which I had last year of taking you for a walk among the beautiful illuminations of Trianon, and I learn with pleasure that you are well, that the little King amuses you and gives you many reasons to be satisfied, kiss him for me. Adieu, mon amie; love him who loves you well.

NAP.

DOROGHOBOYS [DOROGOBUZH], *the 2-th[1] morning*

[1] August 25th.

89

After Dorogobuzh the army continued its advance towards Moscow; the Emperor with Murat, Davout and Ney led the centre, with Poniatowski on the right, and the army of Italy on the left wing. Murat and his cavalry, supported by the Compans Division of Davout's army, followed up the pursuit energetically.

In this hour of crisis the Emperor found in retrospection a moment's respite from his present anxieties. "I look back with regret", he says, "to last year's happiness." On that very day, August 25th, the Empress's fête had been an event of quite exceptional brilliancy. A stormy day had ended in a cloudless night, and the Trianons had been the scene of a splendid gala of music and dancing. The organizers of the fête had made the most of their opportunities; naturally picturesque, the lakes and islands of the park had, under their embellishment, acquired an increase of beauty. A play written by Alissan de Chazet and entitled *The Gardener of Schönbrunn*, had been followed by a ballet at the Trianon Theatre, in which the pick of the artists of the Opera had taken part. The gala had ended with cantatas by Paer, and a banquet.

Now all was changed. Alone, the Empress wandered in the desolate avenues of the Trianons, seeking in vain upon the arid lawns, scorched by the blazing summer, some last faint traces of those better days, of happiness outlived.

Napoleon left Dorogobuzh at 11 p.m., and arrived at the Château de Jaszkhovo, near the Slavkovo outpost, at 5 a.m., on August 27th.

Mon amie

I have received your letter of the 13th, in which I see that my son is slightly ill. I fear that this will cause you anxiety and I hope that he will be promptly cured and that to-morrow I shall know that your worry is over. You see that I am still moving away from you. My health is good, the heat is very great. I love you well. I hope that you will have been satisfied with your journey to Paris and that you will not have had as hot weather as we have here on the 15th of August. Adieu, mon amie. Tout à toi.

NAP.

FROM SLAVKOVO, *the 27th, evening*

He set out again at 11 p.m., and slept in a château on a hilltop some two leagues from Viasma, which he entered on the morning of August 29th.

FROM VIAZMA 29 *Aug*.

Mon amie

I have received your letter of the 14th, in which I saw that the little King had recovered from his fever. I felt sorry for you for the anxiety which it must have caused you; happily it was over quickly. Tell me to-morrow that he has completely recovered. My health is very good; it rained a little last night, which has laid the dust which was choking us and was very incommoding. My affairs are going well. Adieu, mon amie. Tout à toi. Your faithful

NAP.

Viasma, which lies on a tributary of the Dnieper, was an attractive town, and the Emperor obviously enjoyed giving a description of it. For it was there at last that he obtained the supplies of which the army was in need. As a matter of fact the Russians had burnt the bridges and set fire to certain quarters of the town.

Mon amie

I have just received your letter of the 15th of August. You must have been very tired, but I am told that it was not too hot. I am here in a rather fine town, there are 30 churches, 15,000 inhabitants and many shops which sell cognac and other things useful to the army. It has rained a little, which has laid the dust and made the weather cooler. My health is very good. My affairs are going well. Adieu, mon amie. Tout à toi. Your faithful husband

NAP.

I hear that the little King has quite recovered his spirits, kiss him twice for me.

VIASMA 30 *Aug.*

At Velichevo Napoleon gives Marie-Louise to understand that she will be some days without news from him. He is making his preparations for a decisive engagement.

Mon amie

I was pleased to learn that your health was not affected by the fatigue of the 15th and that the little King has no more fever; you must have been anxious, although you knew that it was nothing serious. The fact that you were 2 or 3 days without receiving a courier should not have surprised you for we are far and are moving still further away. My health is good, my affairs are going well. The weather is slightly cooler; it has rained a little. We are now in autumn and no longer in the Dog Days. Adieu mon amie; kiss the little King for me on both cheeks and never doubt your [faithful]

NAP.

VELITSCHEVO 1 *Sept.*, 2 *a.m.*

On September 5th, the Emperor dictates the following bulletin of the Grand Army:

"Deserters, prisoners, inhabitants, are all agreed in stating that the greatest disorder is rife in Moscow and in the Russian Army, which is divided in opinion and has suffered enormous losses. Some of the Generals have been superseded. General Barclay de Tolly is charged with having allowed his divisions to be beaten piecemeal."

This was a fact. A change was made in the High Command. Napoleon was about to meet a foe worthy of his steel.

Mon amie

I have just received your letter of the 17th of August in which I see that the heat has started in Paris; it should last until the 15th of September. My health is good. Here it is autumn. I am pleased with the news which you give me that the little King is quite recovered. Kiss him twice for me. Adieu, mon amie. I think of you and it would give me much pleasure to see you again and to give you a loving kiss. Tout à toi.

NAP.

GHTAL [GHJAT?] 2 *Sept.*

Ma bonne amie

I have just received your letter of the 18th of August. I am pleased to see that you are well and that you are satisfied with the little King. I am very glad that Denon's plan of my campaigns amuses you. You find that I have run into much danger. I have now waged war for 19[1] years and I have given many battles and laid many sieges in Europe,[2] in Asia, in Africa.

I shall hasten to end this one in order to see you and to prove to you the sentiments with which you inspire me. Adieu, mon amie. Tout à toi.

NAP.

GHJAT 2 *Sept. Evening*

Mon amie

I have just received your letter of the 19th. I am leaving to-night to advance in the direction of Moscow. We are in autumn here. We are having the same weather as when we move to Fontainebleau. The granaries are full, the earth is covered with vegetables; consequently the troops are well, which is a great point. My affairs are going well. My health is good. I learn that yours is perfect. Kiss the little King on both cheeks.

Adieu, mio ben.

NAP.

GAT 3 *Sept.*

On September 6th, there comes to Headquarters a carriage with a big packing-case on the box. Baron de Bausset has his name taken in to

---

[1] 16 corrected to 19.

[2] He had first of all written F for *France*, which he altered into *Europe*.

the Emperor: "Sire, I bring you the portrait of the King of Rome." "Have the case opened immediately", orders Napoleon. There then stands revealed a big canvas on which Gérard has recorded the features of *l'Aiglon*. Napoleon is lost in contemplation of the child who is featured as playing cup-and-ball in his cradle, with the terrestrial globe as the ball and an imperial sceptre as the stick. He eventually has the portrait exposed and officers and men file past it— *Morituri te salutant.* It is, indeed, the eve of a bloody battle. With an emotion he strives to master, the Emperor says: "Take him away, it is full early for him to see a battlefield." And he writes:

Ma bonne amie

I am very tired. Baussois has delivered the King's portrait to me. It is a chef d'œuvre. I much appreciate your kind thought. It is as beautiful as you. I shall write to you more fully to-morrow. I am tired. Adieu, mio ben.

Nap.

BORODINO 6 *Sept.*

V

THE BATTLE OF BORODINO

At 2 a.m. on September 7th, standing on the heights of Borodino, Napoleon heartened his army with an inspiriting Order of the Day. "Men, the battle you have desired so keenly is about to begin. Victory depends on you; it will ensure us ample supplies, good quarters and a speedy home-coming. Acquit yourselves like the men you were at Austerlitz and Friedland, at Vitebsk and Smolensk, so that your children's children may say of each of you: 'He fought in the great battle under the walls of Moscow'."

And it was, indeed, one of the bloodiest engagements of the Napoleonic saga. The Emperor had to face an expert tactician, Kutusov, the conqueror of the Turks, on whom the Czar had imposed the task of saving the Russian Empire. And the stately ceremonials of the Orthodox Church had invested the coming conflict with something of the glamour of a Holy War. This is not the place to describe the various phases of this epoch-making battle. Jomini, an eminent strategist of the period, expressed the opinion that in this battle Napoleon failed to display the vigour of conception and execution that had served him at Austerlitz, Friedland and Iena, and he sees as the cause of this a malady from which the Emperor had suffered on several previous occasions. Jomini's surmise is confirmed. "I am very tired", Napoleon wrote on the eve of the Battle of Borodino.

On the morrow of the battle, there left for France a bulletin recording a victory, but in which the Emperor made no secret of the fact that his losses had been heavy—eight generals killed, nine wounded; but as against this, on Colonel Buturlin's own admission, more than fifty thousand Russians were disabled:

> *Ma bonne amie*
>
> I am writing to you on the battlefield of Borodino. I defeated the Russians yesterday, their whole army 120,000 men strong was there. The battle was warmly contested; by 2 o'clock in the afternoon the victory was ours. I made several thousand prisoners and captured 60 guns. Their loss may be estimated at 30,000 men. I had many killed and wounded. Caulincourt, the governor of the pages, has been killed. I had given him the command of a division; I personally was not at all exposed. My health is good, the weather is somewhat cold. Nansouty has been slightly wounded. Adieu, mio bene. Tout à toi.
>
> NAP.
>
> BORODINO 8 *Sept.*

The road to Moscow lay open. Was Kutusov to provide the old capital with a rampart made of

Russian breasts? Having called a council of war, he submitted to his generals the following points: "Should we await the enemy's onslaught on the position held by the Army, or should we evacuate the city without fighting?" Opinions were divided. "Is the preservation of the Army more important for the salvation of the country than that of the capital?" The answer was unanimously in the affirmative.

And Kutusov, falling back on Moscow by the three roads of Mozhaisk, Svenigorod and Kaluga, merely passed through the city without stopping there, for fear of being shut up in it as in a tomb. The Grand Army was at his heels. Napoleon was advancing along the road to Mozhaisk. It was from this small town, and from Tarchi, six leagues from Moscow, that he dated several bulletins sent to the Empress to reassure her about his health.

MOSAISK 9 *Sept.*

Mon amie

I have received your letter of the 24th. The little King, from what you tell me, is very naughty. I received his portrait on the eve of the battle of the Moscova. I had it shown to the army; the whole army thought it admirable, it is a chef-d'œuvre. I feel very chilly through having got caught in the rain at 2 o'clock in the morning whilst visiting our out-posts, but I hope to be rid of this by to-morrow. Besides my health is very good. You can if you wish receive the Prince de Benevent and Rémuzat; there is no objection to it. You can also receive the Bishop of Nantes if he is in Paris. Adieu, mon amie. Tout à toi.

NAP.

Ma bonne amie

I have just received your letter of the 25th. I am grieved to see you sad, I hope that you will let me know to-morrow that you are feeling better. Your father has not received some of your letters. Write to him by courier; it seems that the posts are working badly in Germany. La Valette, to whom you should address your letter, will send it on to him. My health is good; however, I have a slight cold, but it will soon be over. It is very cold here.

NAP.

MOSAISK 10 *Sept.*

Ma bonne amie

I have just received your letter of the 26th. You found the Trianon at its best, for it is the beautiful season of the year. It reminded me of the lovely time you and I spent there together last year; here the heat has ceased, it is cold. My health is good, but I have a slight cold which is coming to an end. My affairs are going well. Kiss the little King twice for me. Write to your father by courier. I am told that he is worried at not receiving news from you. Adieu, mio ben. Tout à toi.

NAP.

The 11*th Sept.*

Mon amie

I have received your letter of the 29th of August. The weather must now be good in Paris; here after a spell of cold weather, it has become milder. My cold is drawing to an end. I beg you to kiss the little King on my behalf. I am 6 leagues from Moscow. Adieu, mio ben. Tout à toi.

TARCHI 13 *Sept.*

NAP.

Mon amie

I have received your letter of the 31st, in which I read that you had received the letters from Smolensk. I have already written to you from Moscow, which I reached on September 14th. The city is as large as Paris, there are 1,600 steeples and more than a thousand fine palaces. The city is provided with everything. The nobility have left, the tradesmen have been compelled to leave as well, the common people have remained. My health is good, my cold has left me. The enemy is retreating as far can be judged towards Kasan. This fine conquest is the result of the battle of the Moskowa. Tout à toi.

NAP.

16 *Sept.*

VI

THE BURNING OF MOSCOW

BUILT on seven hills like Rome, with its two hundred churches and thousand belfries painted every colour, Moscow offered a fascinating spectacle to an observer posted on the heights of Fili. Napoleon set high hope on the occupation of the city; its aristocracy was said to be discontented, rebellious and quite ready to join allegiance with the French.

On September 15th, 1812, with Murat at its head, the Grand Army began its progress through the great city, which General Miloradowitch, with the Russian rear-guard, had only just evacuated. Some volleys of musketry from the Kremlin were silenced by a few rounds of gun-fire. At last, it seemed, the troops would have a welcome spell of rest; what was more, the vast emporia of the city, where the great middlemen of European and Asiatic trade housed their goods, had eight months' stock laid up in them. Then—the fire broke out. It started, so Méneval says, in the Kitaigorod quarter (Chinatown) amongst depots of shawls, furs and Chinese silks. It spread to the Bourse. New fires sprang up at various points. Rostoptschin, the Governor, had

had a number of fire-bombs made, intending to drop them from a balloon on the French troops; now hundreds of incendiaries, splicing them between two strips of wood, began hurling these fire-bombs on to the housetops. The Governor had had all the fire-engines removed, so there was no means of arresting the spread of the fire, despite the severe penalties imposed on incendiaries and the summary execution of three hundred "fire-raisers". Thousands of Russian sick and wounded, abandoned to their fate by Kutusov, perished in the flames.

A "diehard" patriot was the originator of the appalling holocaust—though in a subsequent polemic with Colonel Buturlin he strenuously denied the imputation. The truth was that Rostoptschin, Governor of Moscow, had organized the burning of the city as if it had been a firework display. Yet, so tender-hearted was this man—if we are to believe Countess Chotok—that he refused to attend shooting parties as he "could not bear to kill poor defenceless animals"; he was, it seems, a charming conversationalist, a tender father and adoring husband; it may be noted, however, that Countess Chotok describes his appearance as "repulsive". Such was the man who sacrificed many thousand lives and, as recorded in the *Bulletins de la Grande Armée*, "inflicted on Russia a loss of several milliards of francs". But he had gained his end. Napoleon had intended to strike at the heart of Russia; and all he found, where a great capital had been, was—a heap of stones. His letters to the Empress betray his consternation at this unpredictable disaster, whose magnitude grew daily more apparent to him.

This was one of the rare occasions—perhaps the only one in the Russian campaign—on which the Emperor departed from his wonted imperturbability. When he heard the cries of "Fire!" rising in different quarters of the city, he realized that the burning of Moscow had been deliberately planned. "It's incredible!" he exclaimed in a broken voice, his breast heaving with emotion. "It is a war of extermination, an atrocious form of tactics that has no parallel in the annals of civilization. May the curse of centuries to come fall on the instigators of this act of vandalism!"

Next morning, as Caulaincourt tells us, when the Emperor reviewed his Guard, his face showed "not the faintest trace of the cruel anxieties which had harassed him during the previous night". For Napoleon was a past-master in that royal art —the art of dissimulation. The wearer of a crown —be it a crown of thorns, that lacerates his brow— must smile, smile always! And the brave letters he sent to Marie-Louise after the disaster amply bear this out.

On September 16th, he wrote: "The city is supplied with everything. The nobility have left, the people have remained." But the same day a violent wind fanned the fire; caught in "an ocean of flames, Moscow, one of the richest and most beautiful cities in the world, is no more", stated the *Bulletin de la Grande Armée*, on September 17th. And on the 18th, in his letter to the Empress, Napoleon confirmed the extent of the disaster:

103

Mon amie

I have already written to you from Moscow. I had no conception of this city. It boasted 500 palaces as fine as the Elysée Napoleon, several of them furnished in the French taste with unbelievable luxury, several Imperial palaces, barracks and magnificent hospitals. Everything has been destroyed, consumed by fire for the last 4 days. All the small houses of the bourgeois being of timber, they burn like matchwood. It was the Governor and the Russians, infuriated at their defeat, who set fire to this beautiful city. 200,000 worthy inhabitants are homeless, in misery and despair. There is enough left, however, for the Army, and the Army have found much wealth of every kind, for in this disorder everything is given over to plunder. The loss to Russia is immense and their trade will suffer badly in consequence. The wretches went so far as to remove or destroy the pumps. My cold is at an end, my health is good. Adieu, mon amie. Tout à toi.

NAP.

MOSCOW 18 *Sept.*

Ma bonne Louise

I have received your letter of September 2nd, before you had the news from Smolensk. By this time you will have received those from Moscow. To-day I have been visiting every part of the city. It is a beautiful city; by destroying it Russia has incurred an enormous loss. Only one thousand of the houses are left standing. The troops have found supplies and goods. They have plenty of provisions, and brandy from France. You must not go to the trouble of writing through the Commissioners, for they only arrive 10 days after the couriers. It is a needless and unseemly restraint. You will write only when you have something to say. What you tell me of poor Lucet (?) grieves me. He was a good man. I sincerely pity his wife. Adieu, mon bien.

NAP.

MOSCOW 18 *Sept.*

Practically nothing remained untouched but the Kremlin, in which the Emperor had taken up his abode; the ancient palace of the Czars, with its half-Oriental, half-Slavonic architecture, was full of lofty memories. Napoleon was as much moved by the sight of the throne of Peter the Great as he had been when, in 1806, he visited the study of Frederick the Great at Potsdam. But the whirling flames of the burning city at one time made it impossible to remain at the Kremlin. Not without danger was the Emperor at last induced to leave this fiery furnace. He took refuge at the castle of Petrowsky. His letter of September 20th is dated from Desna:

Mon amie

I am on my way to take up my winter quarters. The weather is splendid, but it cannot last. Moscow being burned to the ground and not being a military position with regard to my ulterior designs, I shall have it abandoned. I shall withdraw the garrison I have left there. My health is good, my affairs are going well. Prince Beauvau was wounded in the thigh by a lance-thrust, he is faring well and was never in any danger; have his mother informed of this by some one of his friends. The occurrence took place in a vanguard skirmish with the Cosaques. My health is good, be cheerful and kiss the little King three times for me. Tout à toi.

NAP.

DESNA 20 *Sept.*

The very same day, the fire having abated, Napoleon was back at the Kremlin, whence a further letter is sent off, to be followed by several others. He makes a show of optimism: "The weather is fine. We have shot so many of the incendiaries, that they have ceased troubling us. My health is very good."

Mon amie

I have received your letter of September 3rd. There is a great deal of rain to-day; they tell me the rainy season is about to set in; fortunately we have arrived. The Army, here, have very good cantonments and barracks. My health is good. Pray be cheerful and in good health. My affairs are going well. Adieu, mon amie. Tout à toi.

NAP.

MOSCOW 20 *Sept.*

Ma bonne amie

I have just received your letter of September 4th. I have written to you every day. I am surprised that you are sometimes a day without hearing from me. What you tell me of the little King gives me much pleasure. I sometimes look at Gérard's portrait, which I think very fine. I suppose you have written to your father. My health is very good. You

From the Painting by Ferdinand Broissard.

THE RETREAT FROM MOSCOW

THE FATAL LETTER TO MARIE-LOUISE
WHICH BLUCHER INTERCEPTED

never mention the Duchess to me; is she in good health?
You must never listen to the idle talk of Paris (?)
Moscow was a very beautiful town, but not a quarter
of the houses are left standing. Adieu, mio ben.
Tout à toi.

NAP.

MOSCOW 21 *Sept.*

Mon amie

I have received your letter of September
7th, written on the day of the battle of the Moscova;
so you are informed by this time of that great event.
All is well here, the heat is moderate, the weather fine.
We have shot so many of the incendiaries that they
have ceased [troubling us]. One quarter of the city
remains, the [other] 3/4 are burned down. My
health is good. Keep in good health, be cheerful,
kiss your son four times for me. All the particulars
you send me about him give me pleasure and make
me very eager to see him. Tout à toi.

NAP.

MOSCOW 23 *Sept.*

On the next day, September 24th, an envoy of
Napoleon's, Iacowieff, left for St. Petersburg
with words of peace: a letter addressed to the
Emperor Alexander opens the door to negotiations. And he possesses his soul in patience.

His thoughts turn to Paris, to Saint-Leu,
to the valley of Montmorency, to the Opera, to
the Comédie Française, the Statutes of which he
draws up, to all the places embellished by the
presence of his dear Louise, *mio bene*, as "her
Nap" calls her in Corsican.

Ma bonne Louise

I have just received your letter of September 8th, in which I read that the weather is very bad in Paris. I have granted what you desire to pay your ladies-in-waiting. My health is very good. The weather is turning rather cold, but a rather spring-like (?) cold. Pray keep well, be cheerful, kiss the little King fondly for me. So the little silly did not recognize his nurse? He is a little wretch! Adieu, mon amie. Tout à toi.

NAP.

MOSCOW 24 *Sept.*

Ma chère Louise

I have received your letter of the 9th, and I am glad to find that you were in very good health, that your son was loveable and was a great source of satisfaction to you. My health is good. Tout à toi.

NAP.

MOSCOW, *the* 25*th*

Mon amie

I have received your letter of September 12th, in which you presume I am in Moscow. You are not mistaken. Everybody speaks well of the little King. I am very desirous of seeing him. Kiss him for me and do not doubt but that I share all your feelings and what you yourself have said, mio ben.

My health is very good. Ton

NAP.

MOSCOW 27 *Sept.*

Mon amie

I have received your letter in which you refer to Saint-Leu. I am very pleased to hear you liked the valley of Montmorency, it is a very picturesque spot, but it is in June that it is at its best. My health is good. I love you. Kiss my son. Tout à toi.

NAP.

MOSCOW 2 *Oct.*

Ma chère Louise

I have received your letter of September 16th, in which you give me such a glowing account of the little King. I was glad to hear you were in good health and easy in your mind. Do be cheerful if you wish to please me, for I could not bear to think you are melancholy and anxious. We shall meet a month earlier or a month later, I am looking forward to this as eagerly as you are, for you do not doubt but that I love you very dearly and that my happiness is to be with ma bonne Louise. Kiss the little King 3 times, love me and never doubt

NAP.

MOSCOW 4 *Oct.* 2 *a.m.*

Ma bien bonne Louise

It gave me great pleasure to read your letter of September 17th. You tell me the new Opera house is very fine. Why have you not been there? It would have amused you. When you do go, have a gratuity given to the author of the libretto, the score and the ballet, provided you are satisfied with these. My health is good. We are having St. Martin's weather here—cold and sunny. Tout à toi.

NAP.

MOSCOW 4 *Oct.* 11 *p.m.*

Napoleon looks back with ever greater longing to the beautiful scenery of the Ile de France, the fine days at Fontainebleau, the warm days of a Paris autumn. And the burning of Moscow only appears to him as a fine panorama to be painted, as interesting as the opera of Baoux-Lormien's *Jérusalem Delivrée*, set to music by Parsuis, the performance of which Marie-Louise had attended on the previous September 15th.

Mon amie

     I have just received your letter of September 18th. I am very sorry to hear you have been slightly indisposed, but I hope it will not have lasted and that I shall hear to-morrow that you are in good health. The weather here is very fine, as warm as in Paris. We have just had fine days like those at Fontainebleau, which has made me look back with regret to that journey on account of the pleasure of being with you. Kiss my son, love me as I love you, il mio dolce amor.

                         Tout à toi.

MOSCOW 6 *Oct.* 2 *a.m.*   NAP.

Ma bonne amie Louise

     I have received your letter of the 19th. I am very glad you were pleased with the panorama of Antwerp. That of the burning of Moscow would be a very fine one to make. Why have you not attended the performance of *Jerusalem* at the Opera House? I am told that opera is very fine and will amuse you. I like to hear you go about. The weather here is very fine, as it is in Paris; it is like a fine day at Fontainebleau. Adieu, mon amie, kiss the little King three times for me and believe in the pleasure it would give me to see you again; you know well that I have no happiness but with you. Write to your father frequently. Send him special couriers; advise him to reinforce *Schwarzenberg's* Corps, so that it may be a credit to him. Adio, mio bene, tout à toi.

NAP.

MOSCOW 6 *Oct.*

Ma bonne Louise

    I have just received your letter of the 20th. I am glad to hear your indisposition had no lasting effects, and that you are in good health. The weather here continues to be splendid, as it is in Paris, beautiful sunshine and not cold, which does a great deal of good. Kiss the little King three times for me, be cheerful and contented. You are quite right to take many walks, it does you good. Adio, mio bene. Tout à toi.

NAP.

MOSCOW 8 *Oct.*

Ma bonne Louise

    I have received your letter of September 22nd. You had just heard of the battle of the Moscova, you will have heard since then of our arrival at Moscow. I deeply sympathize with all your feelings. You know well that I love you as dearly as it is possible to love, consequently all the praises lavished upon you by every one give me great pleasure. I hope the opera *Jerusalem* will have given you a moment's enjoyment. You will tell me whether it is as good as they say it is. I am already grateful to your son for the good he does you and the comfort he is to you. I long as fervently as you do yourself for the time when I shall see you again and be able to tell you all that you know already, how much I love you. Tout à toi.

NAP.

MOSCOW 9 *Oct.*

Ma bien bonne Louise

I have just received your letter of September 29th, and am glad to hear you are well and have entirely recovered your health. All you tell me about my son makes me long to see him. Give him two kisses for me. I observe you people are rather hard to please in Paris; you would like to have the Army Order at once; a few days' interval upsets you. I hope you will have received it the very next day and that you will tell me so in your next letter. I am glad to hear you are pleased, I shall be still more so at seeing you again. It would be very unfair of you, were you to doubt all my love, or suppose my thoughts do not often turn *al mio bene*. Adieu, mon amie. Tout à toi.

NAP.

MOSCOW 11 *Oct.*

Here, for once, a shade of uneasiness is discernible. The Czar's reply does not come to hand, and Marie-Louise is instructed to ask her father for Austrian reinforcements. So intense is his desire to see his wife that the idea begins to take shape in Napoleon's mind of summoning her to Poland.

Ma bonne Louise

My greatest pleasure is to read your letters, it is the first thing I do when the courier arrives. They are charming, as you are yourself, they picture your beautiful soul, and all your noble qualities are to be seen in them. My health is very good. We are having the first snow, yet the weather is not cold.

I do not think you can come to Paris yet and the distance is very great for me to have you come to Poland. Kiss my son 3 times for me. Adio, mio bene.

Tout à toi. NAP.

MOSCOW 14 *Oct.*

Napoleon says nothing of the Council of War which, after a night of anger and anxiety, he convoked on October 3rd; it has, however, been described by General de Ségur.

"Listen to the new plan I have just thought out", he said. "You, Prince Eugène, read. We must burn what remains of Moscow and march by way of Twer on Petersburg, where Macdonald will join us. Murat and Davout will act as our rearguard." The generals present ventured no comment, but their faces betrayed their vast surprise. Then Davout and Daru spoke of the shortage of supplies, the state of the weather, the desolate road they would have to follow. To the Marquis of Caulaincourt, Duc de Vicence, the Emperor suggested a journey to the Czar, for the purpose of opening negotiations. Caulaincourt insisted on the futility of any such attempt. "Alexander will never hear of negotiations until we have completely evacuated Russian territory." "Very well, I will send Lauriston." So Lauriston set out on October 5th with a letter from Napoleon to Alexander. "I want peace; I must have peace! I absolutely insist on it. Let it be honourable— that is all!" Such were his last instructions to his plenipotentiary.

But Napoleon had reckoned without his host,

H   113

without his enemy and without the Russian people. Far from making them eager for peace, the burning of Moscow, which they laid to the account of the French, had inspired the Russians with a passionate craving for revenge; thus, in the past, Nero had saddled the Christians with the odium of the Roman conflagration. The Czar refused to pay the slightest heed to Napoleon's proposals; he even censured Prince Larionowitz for having an interview with the aide-de-camp, General Lauriston. Moreover, Kutusov, while hoodwinking Lauriston with pacific suggestions, entreated the Czar, in the name of the Russian Army, to have no truck with peace proposals.

Then he began to manœuvre for position; by flanking movements he circumvented Murat's outposts, and turned the French positions. Having established himself in the rear of the Grande Armée, he was enabled to get supplies from the southern provinces, whence new recruits were constantly pouring in. Worse, he began to threaten the lines of communication.

Thus it was that one of the Emperor's letters, written at Moscow on October 16th, failed to reach its destination. It was intercepted by the Cossacks, but fortunately told them nothing of the Emperor's intentions.

"My dear, I have received your letter of the 29th. All the agreeable things that people everywhere are saying about you give me much pleasure. I can see you have the gift of pleasing everybody, and that you are greatly loved at Paris. (Otherwise, indeed, they would have to be hard to please!) I hope the little King makes

you very happy. If I am not able to come back
to Paris this winter, I will arrange for you to
come and join me in Poland. Believe me, I am
as eager to see you as you can be, and to tell you
all the feelings you arouse in me. Good-bye, my
dear one. Yours and only yours . . ."[1]

"The mood of lethargy and self-deception in
which Napoleon seemed to acquiesce"—so Jomini writes—"was bound to come to an end, and
the awakening was terrible." Any sort of offensive against St. Petersburg was out of the question.
Could he have proceeded to Volhynia, by way
of Kiev, he would have been able to get fresh
supplies for the army; but, in that case, he would
have had to leave the three army corps on his left
wing at the mercy of the Russians. Napoleon
was in doubt what to do. He recalled the adventure of Charles XII of Sweden, and his hopeless
wanderings in the Russian deserts—for he had
read an account of these in a work by the Swedish
Chamberlain Adlerfeld, *The Military History of
Charles XII*, which was published at Paris in
1741. He had made a point of borrowing it from
the Imperial Library, for he was well aware that
Voltaire's *Life of Charles XII* was little more than
elegant verbiage: "a 'purple passage' of historical
prose, hardly more authentic than the plan of
campaign expounded by Mithridates to his sons
in the eloquent speech Racine has given him in
his famous tragedy."

Napoleon contented himself with returning to
Smolensk by a new route which had not been

---

[1] This is almost the only letter that is not to be found in the
Bibliothèque Nationale.

laid waste by the invading army. The sick and wounded were evacuated to that town from October 15th onwards.

On October 19th, Napoleon informed the Empress that he was going into winter quarters. The one thing which he would not admit, and could not bring himself to write, was that the army was retreating.

Ma chère Louise

     I have received your letter of October 1st. You were perturbed at not having any particulars about my entry into Moscow. I hope you will have had some on the 2nd. You will have observed the folly of these people who have set fire to their own country and thus ruined it for centuries, for Moscow was all the more beautiful and astounding a city in that it was almost the only one of its size in this immense country. Let me hear from you soon that the little King is well and that you are satisfied and more particularly that you are in good health. Adieu, mon amie. Tout à toi. Your faithful and loving husband

MOSCOW 18 *Oct.*   NAP.

Ma bonne Louise

     I am writing to you just before setting out on horseback to visit my outposts. We are having warm weather here, glorious sunshine, as bright as one can have in Paris in October. We have had no cold weather as yet, we have not yet experienced the severity of these northern climes. It is my intention to go into winter quarters shortly and I hope to be able to have you come to Poland so that we may meet. Kiss the little King twice for me and never doubt the feelings of your loving husband

                               NAP.

MOSCOW, *the* 19*th,* 7 *a.m.*

VII

THE RETREAT FROM RUSSIA

THIS was the last day spent at Moscow by the Emperor. Since the previous day the army had been leaving the town uninterruptedly, and a huge column of one hundred and forty thousand men and fifty thousand saddle, draft or pack horses. But if the hundred thousand fighting men on the march in the van with five hundred and fifty guns, still preserved the fear-inspiring appearance of old warriors, the rabble that followed looked like an army of Darius, or a horde of Tartars. There was to be seen, making their way along in three unending files, a confused throng of coaches, gun-limbers, berlins and carts of every description, with trophies of flags and the gigantic Cross of the Great Ivan, with which Napoleon intended to adorn the Dome of the Invalides. Mortier, who covered the retreat, had orders to blow up the Kremlin. This was done on October 23rd.

"A vendetta!" writes Jomini, the severe censor of Napoleon.

Nay, in order to form a fairer opinion of this deed of Napoleon's, read his letters to Marie-Louise.

Ma bonne amie

I have not heard from you these last two days. I have given you warning that I was moving on and that you must not be uneasy should you be three days, as you may be, without hearing from me. My health is good, my affairs are going well. I have left Moscow after blowing up the Kremlin. It would have taken 20,000 men to remain in possession of the city, destroyed as it is; it interfered with my operations. The weather is very fine; it is misty from early morning until two o'clock in the afternoon; then it becomes very fine, and the sun is very warm; in the evening, there is a fine moon until midnight. Such weather is unprecedented. Adio, mio bene, be cheerful and keep in good health. Tout à toi, 3 kisses for the little King.

NAP.

FLOM[IN]KOIE 22 *Oct.*

Ma bonne amie

I have no letters from you for 3 days, because three of my couriers have arrived and are detained at a post, on account of the appearance of a few regulars. I have sent out for them and I shall receive them to-day. My army is on the march. I have had the Kremlin blown up and have departed from Moscow. It did not fit in with my plans to go into winter quarters there. My health is good, the weather is fine, my affairs are going well. Adio, mio bene. Tout à toi.

NAP.

BOROSK, *the* 24*th*, 6 *a.m.*

At Tarontino, Kutusov was unaware of the general retreat of the Grand Army. Under the impression that the IVth Corps of the Viceroy of

Italy, Eugène de Beauharnais, was the only one
on the march towards Borovsk, he had detached
against it the twenty-five thousand men under
Doctorof. But a Cossack having captured an
officer of the Young Guard at the gates of
Borovsk, Doctorof heard that he was running up
against the whole of the Grand Army. And he
determined to forestall the latter at Malojaroslavatz, and gave notice of this at the same time to
Kutusov, who set his troops in motion concur-
rently. Early on October 24th, a furious fight
was started in the streets of Malojaroslavatz, which
was taken and lost no less than seven times in
succession. At the end of the day what was left
of it remained in the hands of the Viceroy,
Eugène. The next day a letter of Napoleon's
addressed to his *dolce amore* announced this
victory without mentioning how costly it had
been for the eighteen thousand French and
Italian troops engaged against fifty thousand
Russians posted above them, without referring to
the humiliation of having had his manœuvre
forestalled and thwarted by an old man, "by a
Scythian"! and without revealing the fact that he
had come within an ace of being carried off by a
party of Cossacks:

Ma bonne amie

I have received your letter of the 9th. All
the particulars you give me about the little King give
me great pleasure, and all you tell me of the sentiments you feel so well because they are sincere and
pure just as you are, are a great comfort to me. If it

were possible my love for you should add to your good qualities. And the regard in which you are held by all is calculated to do so. You will read the news in the Army Order. I am drawing nearer to you and I will think about having you come to Poland if your health allows to bear such a long journey. Adio, mio doulce amore. Tout à toi.

NAP.

BOROVSK 26 *Oct.*

Write to the Vice-Reine that the Viceroy has had a fine fight, that he distinguished himself and that he is in good health.

Ma chère amie

I have received your letter of October 8th. I am glad to hear that you are in very good health. I share your desire to see the end of all this; you must not doubt the happiness it would give me to kiss you; you must not be anxious or worry too much. It may be managed provided your health is good enough. The Viceroy has had a glorious fight, in which he inflicted 5 or 6,000 casualties on the enemy. He is in good health, inform the Vice-Reine of this. Kiss my son twice and never doubt your faithful husband

NAP.

BOROWSK 26 *Oct.*

Between October 26th and November 1st, there is a gap in the Emperor's private letters; these days were some of the most tragic of the retreat. After Malojaroslavatz, both adversaries had fallen back. And all of a sudden there loomed up, with its trees lopped off a few feet from the ground, and its hillocks ravined, a sort of extinguished volcano—a volcano strewn with helmets and cuirasses, broken guns, fragments of uniforms, of blood, stained colours and thousands of dead bodies, half devoured by wolves—the battlefield of Borodino. The Emperor went by quickly and nobody stopped. Here and there, wounded men, who had been left behind and were still alive, held out their hands towards him in supplication.

"The retreat became a rout, an entirely novel sight for Napoleon", wrote his aide-de-camp, Count de Ségur. The Emperor's only thought was now to go into winter quarters in Poland as quickly as possible. And he urged the Empress to obtain reinforcements from her father for Schwarzenberg's Army, which was hard pressed by the Russian Admiral Tchitchagoff and was falling back behind the Bug:

Mon amie   VIASMA *Nov.* 1st

      You will see by the date of this letter that I am nearing Poland in order to establish my winter quarters there. There will thus be 100 leagues fewer between us. The weather is splendid, 3 or 4 degrees below freezing point, glorious sunshine. My health is perfect, my affairs in good shape. All I lack is the happiness of seeing you and telling you how I love you. Kiss the little King for me. Write to your father that I request him to remember Schwarzenberg, to have him supported by the Corps in Gallicia, and to reinforce him. When you write to the Empress, tell her I am at her feet. Adieu, mon amie. You know how I think of you. Tout à toi.

NAP.

Mon amie

I have just received your letter of October 18th. I was very sorry to hear of the death of the little Prince of Baden. His mother will be greatly distressed, it is a very painful occurrence, particularly for a mother. As soon as I have gone into winter quarters, I will have peace signed in order to keep my promise. You must not doubt but that I shall be desirous as you yourself to meet you, for you know how I love you. My health is good, the weather is glorious, slightly cold, with very fine sunshine. I am drawing nearer to you every day, and as soon as things are settled I will write to you. Meanwhile, as I know you are very reasonable, I trust you will mind not to be uneasy, but cheerful, contented and keep from worrying, which would grieve me too much. Kiss my son 3 times for me and never doubt all the very loving feelings with which you inspire me. Your faithful husband   NAPOLEON

VIASMA 2 *Nov.*

And here is what the name of Viazma and the date of November 2nd stand for. While Napoleon is silent here as regards the military operations, the *Bulletin de la Grande Armée* is more informative:

"Ever since the fighting at Malojaroslavatz, the vanguard had not caught sight of the enemy, save for the Cossacks, who, like the Arabs, hang about our flanks and annoy us by sniping.

"On November 2nd, at 2 p.m., 12,000 Russian infantry, covered by a swarm of Cossacks, cut the road, at a distance of one league from Viazma, between the Prince of Eckmühl and the Viceroy.

The Prince of Eckmühl and the Viceroy ordered this column to be attacked, drove it off the road into the woods. . . . Since then the Russian infantry has not been seen, but only the Cossacks."

This is what had happened: the Viceroy, Eugène de Beauharnais, was close to Viazma, but the Prince of Eckmühl, Davout, had not got beyond Federowskoï, where Miloradowitch, "the Russian Murat", debouched between them: caught as between the two claws of a pair of tweezers, he received reinforcements which enabled him momentarily to occupy Viazma, so that both adversaries claimed to have been victorious.

There is no reference to this fighting in the letters of the next day, except: "My affairs are going well. In a few days' time we shall be in position." And he is already turning his attention to the enchanting place whereat he might receive Marie-Louise and her father in Poland:

Mon amie

I have received your letter of the 19th. I was glad to read the favourable account you give me of the state of your health and that of my son. We are having very fine weather here, bright sunshine with temperature 2 or 3 degrees below freezing point. This is very helpful with regard to our movements. We shall have taken up our position in a few days' time. You will be very pleased to find we are 100 leagues nearer, you were fearing lest I should be moving away still farther. My affairs are going well. My health is perfect. Take care of yourself and keep well. Kiss the little King twice for me. Tout à toi.

NAP.

HALF-WAY FROM VIASMA TO DOROGOBUSCH 3 *Nov.*

Mon amie

I have just received your letter of October 20th. I am expecting you to inform me at any moment that my son has cut his teeth and the slight distemper that has been trying his health is a thing of the past. The weather keeps very fine. My health is perfect; such an autumn is unheard of—bright sunshine and only 2 or 3 degrees below freezing point—this makes marching easy and not fatiguing. Pray write often to your father and to Vienna. Supposing you were to come to Poland, would your father wish to come and see you there for a few days? Adio, mio bene. Tout à toi.

NAP.

3 *Nov.*

Ma bonne amie

I have received your letter of October 22nd. It would have given me as much pleasure as to youself to make the journey to Fontainebleau, but it is no longer to be thought of this year, that of next year will be all the pleasanter. I hope you will soon inform me that my son has cut his teeth and recovered his good temper. The weather is still fine here. But I think it will be bad before long. My health is very good. Tout à toi.

NAP.

5 *Nov.*

Very different from the preceding letters was the Imperial missive penned on November 7th, at 1 a.m., which betrays both anxiety and discontent: discontent with the Minister of War, anxiety for Marie-Louise. . . .

The remains of the Grand Army were dragging along, soaked to the skin, and shivering. Their strength failing them, men would fall down, to be soon covered up by the snow. In this "dying army trudging through natural surroundings that were dead", to quote General de Ségur, a man trudged along, with a stick in his hand, and clad in a fur-lined coat and Astrakhan bonnet. It was the Emperor. He was arm-in-arm with the King of Naples, when Count Daru brought him a letter from the Empress. What did she write? She was living quietly at Saint-Cloud when a detachment of the Guard rushed into the court-yard of the château. In her dressing-gown, her hair dishevelled, she hastened out on to the balcony, in a state of extreme agitation. The Emperor was reported to be dead and the Empire to have come to an end. Everybody is unnerved: Cambacérès, Savary, Pasquier, Hulin, the Arch-chancellor, the jurists, the Prefect of the Seine Department, all take the news to be true without verifying it. Yet an old adjutant, Laborde, has his doubts. He has recognized an ex-prisoner. And very soon the guilty party, General Malet, is arrested with his accomplices. The fact remains, none the less, that alone, without money or credit, a man who had been in prison came very near to bringing down the pillars of the Empire. This it is to which reference is made in a letter of the Emperor's, written in a house surrounded by a palisade, which had served as a post office. It affords no inkling of the fact that the news had so deeply affected the Emperor that it was not long before he left behind the remnant of the Grand Army and returned post-haste to Paris.

Mon amie

I have received your letter of October 23rd. I am sorry the Minister of War sent an aide de camp to you about the soldiers who offended Hulin. He should have informed the Duchess or Baussois of the affair. All this, I fear, will have upset you, though I know your disposition. You see I am drawing closer. To-morrow I shall be at Smolensk, or more than 400 leagues nearer Paris. The weather is beginning to show signs of impending snow.

My health is good. I read your letters with as much pleasure as you can have in reading mine. Henceforward I shall receive yours in 12 days, instead of 17. When the sledge transport (?) has come in and I have taken up my winter quarters, I shall receive them in 8 or 10. Adieu, ma bonne Louise, kiss my son twice and above all never doubt all the love I bear you. Tout à toi.

NAP.

7 Nov. 11 *a.m.*

Napoleon follows the devastated road that leads to Smolensk, which he reaches on November 9th. In summer, the town had struck him as charming, and its environs rich and abounding in cereals. What a disappointment! Instead of resources, he finds nothing but scenes of desolation: thousands of sick and wounded have been brought here. Supplies were almost exhausted. Vanished in thin smoke were the promised land, the expected manna. And two further enemy armies were hastening up to cut off the retreating army. It was necessary to hasten away before the last avenue to safety was closed. On the 14th,

SOULT

(Nicolas Jean de Dieu Soult, Duke of Dalmatia,
Marshal of France, 1769-1851.)

NEY WITH THE REAR-GUARD

the Emperor left Smolensk, leaving to Ney the duty of blowing up the city walls. The situation was getting worse. Of this, not a word from Napoleon to Marie-Louise:

Mon amie
      I have received your letter of October 29th. It gives me pleasure to see you are satisfied with the French and that you esteem them. As for myself you think altogether too highly of me, but that is the effect of your partiality, which I value very much for my happiness is bound up with your sentiments. You know well how fondly attached to you I am on my part. Kiss my son, I long to see him; he will, by that time, be very big and very good, I hope. Adio, mio bene. Tout à toi.

NAP.

SMOLINSK 12 *Nov.*

Ma bonne amie
      I have just received your letter of the 30th. I see you have been to the Salon; tell me what you think of it; you are a connoisseur, for you paint pretty well. The cold here is pretty sharp—8 degrees below freezing point, which is rather lucky. My health is very good. Kiss my son, tell me how he is getting on with his teething. Adio, mio bene.

NAP.

SMOLENSK 14 *Nov.*

The next letter is dated from Orcha (Orsha). A mere allusion to the raids of the Cossacks. As a matter of fact, the break-up is beginning. A Proclamation issued at Orcha on November 19th admits the sad truth: "A great many of you have deserted your colours and proceed alone, thus betraying their duty, the honour and safety of the Army. Such disorders must come to an end. . . . Offenders will be put under arrest and punished summarily." On that day, Napoleon consigned to the fire all the papers he had collected with a view to writing the history of his life. And now let us read his letter to Marie-Louise.

Ma bonne amie

The Cossacks have swooped down upon our communications, which prevents me from hearing from you, but I will not lose a moment before writing to you. I am in good health and drawing nearer to you. In a few days' time, communications will be opened up. Adio, mio bene. Tout à toi.

Nap.

Orcha 20 *Nov.*

Pass on the news to the Queen of Naples and the Vice-Reine. Show my letter to the Archchancellor.

VIII

THE CROSSING OF THE BERESINA

EVEN in the darkest hours of the campaign, Napoleon never failed to write to Marie-Louise. Indeed, there could be no better evidence of his fortitude of spirit than the letters written at the time of the crossing of the Beresina. The Beresina, its banks deep-set with marshes, lay before him; the further bank was held by Admiral Tchitchagoff. The French flank was threatened by Wittgenstein, who was marching down from the north along the left bank of the river. Behind was Kutusov. The army was hemmed in, caught in a trap, and the sole way of escape led over the one bridge spanning the Beresina at Borisov. The Dombrowski division which held it was dislodged by the Russian Admiral, and fell back on Oudinot on November 21st. Oudinot sent a despatch from Bohr to inform the Emperor of this disaster. No news could have been more tragic, more discouraging. Who could guess from a reading of Napoleon's letter to the Empress that on that very day at Bohr, he had given orders for the burning of the Eagles, lest they should be left as trophies for the enemy.

Mon amie

     I have had no letters from you for many days, but to-morrow or the day after I shall receive them all at once, the road having been cut. The weather is cold. You must have been very anxious at not hearing from me for several days. My health is very good. Kiss the little King for me and never doubt the sentiments of your faithful husband

NAP.

BOHR 24 *Nov.*

The King of Naples, the Viceroy, the Prince de Neufchâtel, the Marshal and my Household are all in good health.

A charge by Oudinot's troops led by Marbot's *chasseurs*, put them in occupation of Borisov once again, but could not prevent the Russian Grenadiers, covered by the batteries, at the bridge-head, from burning down the bridge. Happily, the Emperor was now informed by two Cavalry Generals, Colbert and Corbineau, that there was a ford two leagues away, at Studienka. The Cavalry crossed the ford. Naval pontoniers and sappers built two open trestle bridges at this spot on November 26th; one of them served for the Artillery, the other for the Infantry. These bridges were the salvation of the army. On that day, and the next, the army marched past under the Emperor's eyes. And, as though the imminence of supreme disaster had left his mind untroubled by the least qualm of anxiety, Napoleon wrote to Marie-Louise:

Ma bonne amie

You will have been many days without receiving any letters from me; I am afraid you must have been very anxious. The Duc de Bassano, at least, will have brought you some news. I am nearing the time when I shall receive all your letters. My health is very good, the cold is very great. Adieu, mon amie, you know how deeply I love you. Give the Queen of Naples, the Vice-Reine, the Princesse de Neufchâtel, news of their husbands, who are in good health. Tout à toi.

NAP.

On the night of the 27th the Emperor slept in a humble hut at Zaniwski. His suite were lodged in a single room, herded promiscuously together like sheep in a pen. Next day, at 7 a.m., a twofold attack was launched against the army; by Wittgenstein against Maréchal Victor on the left bank, by Tchitchagoff against Oudinot, Ney and Dombrowski on the right bank. Napoleon remained with the Guard which was massed at Brilowa in reserve, defending the two bridge-heads. The Russian Admiral was defeated; Wittgenstein continued his attack till the following day. Of the tumult of this battle we do not catch the faintest echo in the letter sent to Marie-Louise from the little town of Zembin (Sembin) in the centre of a swamp crossed by the Vilna road:

Ma bonne amie

I know that 15 couriers are awaiting me at a distance of three days' march. I shall thus find 15 of your letters there. I am much worried at thinking of the sorrow it will give you to be so many days without hearing from you, but I know that on extraordinary occasions I must rely on your courage and strength of character. My health is perfect, the weather very bad and very cold. Adieu, ma douce amie; two kisses to the little King from me. You know all the tenderness of the sentiments of your husband.

NAP.

ZEMBIN 28 *Nov.*

The King of Naples, the Viceroy, the Prince de Neufchâtel are in good health—give news of them to their wives—as well as the Grand Marshal, who is writing, and all my aides-de-camp. Also give news of her son to Madame Montesquiou.

The Beresina has been crossed—but at what a cost! The Partouneaux Division has been sacrificed, at Borisov, to cover the retreat. The bridges were cut behind Maréchal Victor's army corps, the last to cross the river. The motley crowd of followers was thus cut off: disbanded soldiers, stragglers, thousands of men of every arm, in tattered uniforms with hardly human faces and hollow cheeks, the miserable jetsam of a great retreat. Captivity awaited them. But what hint of this tragic scene is to be found in the Emperor's letter sent from Illia?

Mon amie

The 20 couriers who are missing will, I hope, reach me to-morrow, when I shall have news of you, which I very much long to receive. I have written to you by express messengers. The weather is very cold, my health is very good. Be cheerful and contented. Your wishes will be granted sooner than you think. Give two kisses to my son and never doubt the loving sentiments of your faithful husband

NAP.

ILLIA 1 *Dec.*

Mon amie

I am sending you Montesquiou, who will give you news of the Army. He will tell you how well I am and above all how much I love you. Adio, mio bene. Tout à toi.

NAP.

NEAR MOLODETSCHNO 2 *Dec.*

Ma bonne amie

Yesterday I sent you Anatole Montesquiou, who will give you news of this country. I thought you would be very glad to see some one to whom you can talk of what interests you. Now the regular courier will leave in an hour's time. I will answer twenty of your letters, for I am expecting 20 couriers in an hour's time. Adio, mio bene. Ton

NAP.

MOLODETSCHNO 3 *Dec.*

The "News of this Country"—too terrible to bear writing of—is nevertheless recorded on the same day, and at the same place, Molodetschno (Mlodzieczno), in the *Bulletins de la Grande Armée.* This is the most tragic of all the records of the Russian campaign. The thermometer has fallen many degrees below zero, the horses have died by thousands. With cavalry inadequate to cover the army or act as scouts at a greater range than a quarter of a league, unable to join battle for lack of artillery, the army plods on and on. Their heads are bowed, all gaiety has left them; they are continually harassed by Cossacks who would be incapable of pressing an attack home against a company of skirmishers. Not a few are taken prisoner by these Cossack bands. So urgent is the danger that a "sacred squadron", consisting of four companies with Grouchy in command, has been formed, mounted on the last surviving horses; its Captains are Generals, its non-commissioned officers, Colonels: it is the Emperor's bodyguard, his ultimate defence.

Meanwhile the author of the *Soirées de Saint-Pétersbourg*, who personally witnessed the Russian triumph, was drawing philosophical conclusions from these events. "There is something miraculous about what is happening to-day", thus Joseph de Maistre wrote to the Baronne de Pont. "Napoleon entered Russia with four hundred thousand men and a thousand guns at least. Men and cannon, all have vanished away. At the present moment there are a hundred and fifty thousand prisoners. A gigantic monument is being planned, to be erected at Moscow. It will be wrought in 'captive bronze', as ancient inscriptions put it. I commend to your admiration this man who never convened a Council of War, who boasts, what is more, that he never took any man's advice, and on this occasion had the notion of convening three Councils of War— merely in order to contradict them. That, Madame, was his ruin, but our salvation."

Mon amie

I have just received your letter of the 24th.
I am much distressed at all the anxiety you are going
through which will last another fortnight at least.
My health, however, has never been better. You
will have seen in the Army Orders that things have
(not ?) gone as well as I would have wished, yet
affairs are not going badly just now. The weather is
bitterly cold. In a few days' time I shall make up my
mind about your journey for the purpose of meeting
again soon. Live in hope and do not worry.

Adio, mio bene. Tout à toi.

N.

5 Dec.

"Affairs are not going badly just now." What
is to be understood thereby? On that day,
December 5th, at headquarters at Smorgony
(Smorghonie) the Emperor assembled the chief
leaders of the Army in view of an important
communication: the King of Naples, Murat, is
to take over, with the rank of Lieutenant-General,
the supreme command of the Army, or the ghost
of an army.

As for himself, the Emperor will vanish in the
course of the night. Incognito, under the name
of Duc de Vicence, so that no one may be
tempted to hold the unsuccessful warrior as
hostage, he travels by way of Vilna, Warsaw,
Dresden, Leipzig and Mayence; he is on his way
to Paris, where a post-chaise lands him on
December 18th.

"I had gone to fight men in arms, not angry

135

Nature", he observed in his exile at St. Helena. "I defeated their armies. But I was unable to conquer fire, frost, numbness and death. Fate was stronger than I!"

Well, in Paris he has joined his *doux amour*, his *bene*, his *bonne Louise*, who, it must be stated plainly, had lived in anguish from one end of the campaign to the other. "A single day without a letter suffices to drive me to despair", she wrote to her friend, Victoire de Poutet, whom she told of her joy after Napoleon came back: "I am sure you will share the happiness it has given me to have him back after an absence of seven months."

IX

THE CAMPAIGN IN GERMANY

THE SPRING CAMPAIGN——THE VICTORY

LEFT at the head of the last remnant of the Grand Army, Murat had departed on January 17th, 1813, for Italy, there to restore his tottering fortunes. Though it would have been equally to his interest to leave, the Viceroy of Italy, Eugène de Beauharnais, remained where duty called: he did not forsake the phantom army, but took over the command.

As a consequence of the disaster on the Beresina, Macdonald, in the north, evacuated Courland. He had two Prussian Divisions as a rear-guard. After a parley with the Russians, the Prussian Generals Yorck and Massenbach signed a convention of neutrality with them on December 30th, 1812. Though the King of Prussia, Frederick William, refused to subscribe to this action, they remained just the same at the head of their troops.

Developments followed apace. On March 1st, 1813, Prussia signed a treaty of alliance with Russia. A mass of proclamations flooded Germany, inflaming the spirit of hatred and revenge.

"To arms!" shouts Blücher. "Let the standards be raised against the oppressor." "Let every German assist in our plans of liberation!" cries Kutusov. And Wittgenstein, in order to stir up the Saxons, calls up the memory of another Emperor: "Charles the Great was his name. He made war on you. Witikind was your King. He did not urge you to keep still . . ."—an allusion to the behaviour of the wandering king, Frederick Augustus, who refused to desert the cause of France.

On March 9th, the Viceroy, Eugène de Beauharnais, was in position behind the Elbe, with his headquarters at Leipzig, his left at Madgeburg, his right at Dresden: Wittgenstein's troops debouch from Berlin and march towards Magdeburg; Kutusov, Wintzingerod and Blücher coming from Silesia march towards Dresden, which General Reynier is compelled to leave on March 26th. Many French garrisons are still holding out at Hamburg, Bremen, Stettin, Danzig, etc. . . .

Napoleon hastens to take personal command of the armies in Germany. On March 30th, 1813, in the Throne Room, in presence of the high dignitaries of the Empire, he invests with the Regency the Empress, who takes the oath. He leaves to the Arch-chancellor Cambacérès the care of reading the police reports, which are sometimes numerous: "One should not defile the mind of a young woman". To his allies, the Dukes of Baden and Würzburg, the Kings of Wurtemberg, Bavaria and Saxony, he sends

instructions to prepare their contingents. And
at four o'clock on April 15th, he sets out, writing
notes on his way, and passing through Sainte-
Menehould, Mars la Tour and Mayence:

Ma bonne Louise

I have just reached Sainte-Menehould, at
8 o'clock, in time for dinner. I have had a fine day.
I was sad at leaving you and very anxious to hear
from you. Enjoy yourself, be cheerful, it is vital to
your health. Adieu, mon amie, mille choses aimables.
Tout à toi.

NAP.

15th, 8 p.m.

Ma bonne Louise

I arrived here at Midnight on the 16th, so
I was less than 40 hours on the way. I wrote you a
few lines from the place at which I stopped. My
health is very good. I have had no letters from you
to-day. I long to hear how you are and what you have
been doing. Tell me you have been good and that
you are brave. I have a great deal of work, as you
may suppose. The Grand Marshal has not reached
here yet. Adieu, ma douce amie. A kiss from me to
the little King.

NAP.

MAYENCE 17th, 6 p.m.

The trite remark that he has had the Grand
Duchess of Baden, Stéphanie-Napoléonne, wife
of the Grand Duke Charles-Louis-Frederick, to
dinner, the teasing allusion to the fickleness of the
weaker sex, are in glaring contrast with the

139

gravity of the recommendation to give military details to "Papa François", whom it is needful to impress, with a view to keeping his alliance.

Ma bonne et douce amie

I have received your letter of the 15th. It touched me deeply, it is full of all sorts of kind and sweet thoughts. I am very anxious for you to cheer up and be in good health, you know how necessary that is for my happiness. Kiss my son on the eyes. Write to Papa François once a week, send him military particulars and tell him of my affection for his person. My health is perfect. I have been in the saddle all day seeing to my fortifications. The whole army is on the move. Adieu, ma bonne Louise, love me as I love you, provided such a thing is possible to *one of your versatile sex*. Tout à toi. Ton époux

18 [*April*], 2 *p.m.* NAP.

Ma bonne amie

I have just received your letter of the 16th. I am sorry to hear that your health is not as good as I would wish it to be, and that you contribute to make it unsatisfactory by worrying. I had the Duchess of Baden to dinner yesterday. I am in very good health. It is very windy here. I think of you and wish you to tell me that you are well. A kiss to your son. Tout à toi. NAP.

[MAYENCE] 19 [*April*], 2 *p.m.*

Ma bonne Louise

I have received your letter with the news of my son. I expect the two lozenges had something to do with the trouble he took to remember me. I will not have you suffer from your digestion; cheer up and you will be well. The affairs of State will give you a certain amount of pleasure. That will do you good. I am in the best of health. Adieu, mon amie. Tout à toi.

N<small>AP</small>.

20 [*April*], 9 *p.m.*

Ma douce Louise

I have received your letter; would that I were with you. The habit of seeing you and spending my life with you is very sweet. I am sorry to hear what you tell me about the little King. I do hope he will have recovered his usual appetite. Write and tell me he is in good health. The weather here is pretty fine, I shall stay a few days longer. There has been a slight affair in the streets of Weimar; a regiment of Prussian hussars was cut off and some fifty men taken prisoners, including one of Blüker's aides-de-camp. It is not worth mentioning. Adio, mio bene.

N<small>AP</small>.

M<small>A</small>[YENCE] 21*st*

For the first time there now appears under Napoleon's pen, the name of the redoubtable Prussian General who will later on be responsible for his ultimate defeat: Blücher. At Weimar, the Emperor has paid his respects to a lady who, he opines, boasted "the head of a great man", Louise of Hesse-Darmstadt, the wife of the Grand Duke Charles Augustus of Saxe-Weimar.

Ma bonne Louise

I cannot conceive how a day has passed without your receiving a letter from me. I see by your letter of the 19th that the little King is up to his old tricks. I do long to hear that you are in perfect health. Love me for you know how I love you. Tout à toi.

NAP.

[MAYENCE *April*] 22*nd*, 7 *p.m.*

Ma chère Louise

The weather is very bad to-day, which has given me a slight cold. I have been coughing, but I hope it will be all over by to-morrow morning. There is a difference of 15 degrees between Paris and this place. I am glad to hear the little King is so lovable and that he loves you. I fancy he has quite forgotten me, though Madame de Montesqu[lou] writes to the contrary. Give him two kisses for me. You must have heard from Vienna; there have been couriers. I think I shall be leaving for Erfurt to-morrow. My affairs are taking shape. The King of Saxony has proceeded to Prague, in order to be nearer home. There has been some slight skirmishing to our advantage between the Elbe and the Weser. Adieu, mon amie. Tout à toi. Ton époux

NAP.

MA[YENCE] 23 *April*

"My affairs are taking shape." On reaching Mayence with his Grand Equerry, Louis de Caulaincourt—whose brother had been killed at Borodino—he had found moral confusion. The most absurd news was circulated in secret. The whole of Westphalia was in the grip of anxiety. But at Mayence, "as is everywhere and always the case, the Emperor was a talisman which restored the morale of the Administration, and made people easy in their minds." To this impression, four regiments of the Old Guard, who were reviewed by the Emperor, contributed their prestige. General Curial arrived with the cadres of twelve others. The utmost haste, however, was necessary: the war bulletins addressed to the Empress Regent made no secret of the fact that Thorn had surrendered, that Danzig was threatened, that Stettin, Custrin, Glogau and Spandau, still garrisoned by the French, were blockaded, that the garrison of Wittemberg had forcibly repulsed an assault.

Just before leaving Mayence, on April 24th, at 8 p.m., to take the field, Napoleon sends Marie-Louise an extremely important letter.

Ma chère Louise

I have received your letter of the 21st. I am surprised at Papa François saying that peace depends on myself, when for the last four months he has been unable to obtain an answer and her (Russia's) consent to open negotiations. Write to him to that effect, tell him it is wrong to pretend that it is I who do not want peace when he has not yet consented to open negotiations, but that if they want to impose conditions upon me without negotiating a surrender, they are very far out in their reckoning. Ask him to be mindful lest the aim of all this be to drag him into the war, for after all, if peace is what is wanted, negotiations must be entered upon. Now I told him

3 months ago that I was prepared to do so, to which
he made no answer. Let him see, Louise, that this
country is not going to allow Russia and England to
bully her or impose shameful conditions upon her, and
while I now have a million men under arms, I could
have as many as I choose, if the French knew that it is
intended to sacrifice us to the fury of the English.
Forward your letter through the Austrians to ensure
its secrecy. My health is very good, though the
weather here is very cold. Adieu, mon amie. Tout
à toi.
                                                    Nap.

MAYENCE 24 *April*

Ma bonne Louise

   I shall leave here to-night at 9 o'clock for
Erfurt, where I shall be to-morrow, the 25th, but the
letter I shall write to you will be delayed thereby for
a day or two. My health is very good. Kiss the little
King for me.   I was glad to hear that Madame Mont
[esquiou] was well again.   Adieu, mon amie, it grieves
me to be away from you. Tout à toi.
                                                    Nap.

MAYENCE 24 *April*

Ma bonne amie

   I have arrived at Erfurt safe and sound in
22 hours. I am writing just a line to you before
going to bed. Adieu, mon amie.
                                                    Nap.

ERFURT 25*th*

Erfurt! what happy memories clung to the
place: in this pleasant town of Saxony, over which
the Thuringerwald casts its shadow, Napoleon

144

had erstwhile received Goethe. Here, too, in 1808, he had assembled a host of Kings in a peaceful congress, to which, as a welcome interlude, was afforded a feast worthy of the gods—the performance of *La Mort de César* with Talma in the title part. In *Œdipe*, the words: "the friendship of a great man is a gift of the gods", were greeted with frantic applause, so warm was the affection of Czar Alexander for Napoleon; whereas now! . . .

Now, Napoleon is reviewing at Erfurt the Guard and a Division of the VIth Corps before marching against Alexander. From every depot throughout the Empire, by countless routes, a host of men assemble at the meeting-place appointed by the Emperor, who now has a large army at his disposal.

Ma bonne amie

    I have just received your letter of the 23rd. I am glad to hear you are taking physic in order to recover your health. The little King is well, he is a comfort to you. My health is very good. My affairs are going well. The weather is splendid. I love you and I am sure you are not aware of it. Pray write to Papa François not to let himself get entangled. Adieu, mon amie. Tout à toi.

NAP.

ERFURT 27*th*, 6 *p.m.*

In Paris, Napoleon had left Schwarzenberg, his comrade in arms in Russia, making the following appointment to meet him: "By the beginning of May, I shall be in person on the right bank of the Elbe, with three hundred thousand men; Austria might raise your army in Cracow to one hundred and fifty thousand men, meantime assembling thirty or forty thousand men in Bohemia; and on the day of my arrival on the Elbe, we could all debouch simultaneously against the Russians. That is the way in which we shall succeed in pacifying Europe." Thereupon, he hastened his departure for Mayence.

Schwarzenberg had not dared to say "No" to the Emperor. But in presence of the weak Marie-Louise, and of Maret, Duc de Bassano, he lays stress upon the passions raised in Europe against France and the impossibility for Austria to take up arms against Germany. And contrary to Napoleon's expectation, Austria withdraws her contingent. This was but the first step towards other destinies.

Ma bonne amie

I am writing just a few lines. I have received your letter of April 25th. On the 29th, yesterday, we had a successful little affair at the small town of Vesenfeld [Weissenfels]. General Souham, with his Division, overthrew a Russian Division, 5 to 6,000 strong, and killed a great many of them. My health is good. I shall sleep at Veselfeld to-night. I have joined hands with the Viceroy, who is at Mersebourg. Adieu, mio bene. Tout à toi.

NAP.

NAUMBURG 30 *April*

Souham, in command of Ney's rearguard, was on the march towards Weissenfels, when at 2 p.m., on April 29th, he was confronted by a Russian Division under Lanskoi. Though having no cavalry, he overthrew and battered it with his twelve guns, supported by sharpshooters posted in ravines. The charges of the Russian Cavalry were broken by the French Battalions who had formed square. And as the Russians still clung to the little town of Weissenfels, Souham's men charged them, bearing their shakos on the end of their guns, and dislodged them, shouting "Vive l'Empereur!" Napoleon made his entry the next day into the captured townlet.

Mon amie

I have received your letter of April 26th. I am glad to hear your health is very good. There was great deal of rain here yesterday, and it disagreed with me. Now the sun is shining. I am just riding off. Give two kisses to my son. Adio, mio bene. Tout à toi.

NAP.

VESENFELD 1 *May*, 10 *a.m.*

Ma bonne amie

I have just received your letter. You can acknowledge receipt of the Archchancellor's letter the first time. After that, you will have your letters written by the Archchancellory, to whom you will send his reports. You can have a letter written to Madame de Montesquiou, telling her that the next time there is an appointment of ladies in waiting, her name will be put before me. Write and tell Papa

François not to allow himself to be led away by the hatred his wife bears us, that it would be fatal to himself and a source of many calamities. I was sadly grieved at the death of the Duke of Istria, it was a great shock to me. He went out with the skirmishers without any good reason, partly out of curiosity, the first cannon-ball killed him outright. Have some message sent to his poor wife. My health is very good. Have the Vice-Reine informed that the Viceroy is in good health. Adieu, mon amie. Tout à toi.

NAP.

LÜTZEN 2 *May*

Napoleon left Weissenfels on May 1st at 9 a.m. On his way to Lützen he had a skirmish with Wintzingerod at Pozerna. The affair was prompt and successful. From a height, field-glass in hand, Marshal Bessières, Duke of Istria, wrapped in his cloak, was watching the retreat of the Russians, when a cannon-ball knocked him over. "A very great loss!" exclaimed Napoleon. "Bessières deserved to die like Turenne. An enviable death."

As for the Empress of Austria, whose hatred had not abated, Napoleon had a surprise ready for her by the next day:

Ma bonne amie

It is eleven at night; I am very tired. I have gained a complete victory over the Russian and Prussian armies under Emperor Alexander and the King of Prussia. I lost 10,000 men, killed and wounded. My troops covered themselves with glory and proved their love in a way that went to my heart. Kiss my son. I am in very good health. Adieu, ma bonne Louise. Tout à toi.

NAP.

[*undated*] LÜTZEN 2 *May* 1813

Ma bonne amie

I am sending you particulars of the battle. Have them inserted in the *Moniteur*. My health is very good. The whole of my household are well. One of my orderly officers, Bérenger, was struck by a bullet which wounded him slightly. Adieu, mon amie, write in Italian by telegraph.

NAP.

PEGAU (?) 4 *May*

An official despatch, dated May 2nd, informed the Queen-Empress and Regent of the details of the Battle of Lützen. The Czar and the King of Prussia, hearing that the French Army was debouching from Thuringia, moved forward to confront it and take up strong positions. But this scheme was frustrated by the rapidity of the advance.

On May 2nd, the French Army was advancing through the plain, with its left wing, under Prince Eugène, resting on the Elster; its centre, under Ney, was at Kaia, while Napoleon with his Guard occupied Lützen. Lauriston, on the extreme left, swerved in the direction of Leipzig, in order to confuse the enemy. While the armies of the Allies were debouching, in deep columns, on Kaia, Napoleon swung his army round, crossed to the right bank of the Elster, and took the enemy in the rear. Ney held his own against furious onslaughts at the village of Kaia, which was taken and retaken several times. At the moment when the Russians and Prussians were heavily engaged, General Bertrand launched an attack on their rear. The battle was won. The French occupied the heights whence the Czar and the King of Prussia had watched the battle. Owing to the lack of cavalry, the pursuit of the defeated enemy could be carried on for a distance of only one and a half leagues. "Maman Beatrice", the Austrian Empress—what cold and calculated irony lies in these appellations!—was invited to take cognizance of the Bulletin announcing this victory which Napoleon sent to Marie-Louise. And, as it turned out, the Court of Vienna, startled by the turn of events and apprehensive, presently sent Metternich to pay his compliments to the French Ambassador, and, after that, despatched a plenipotentiary to the victor. In dealing with "Papa François", Napoleon had recourse to methods of intimidation.

Ma bonne amie

I have received your letter of April 30th. I was rejoiced to hear what you tell me of my son and of your health. Mine is very good. The weather is very fine. I am pushing on in pursuit of the enemy, who has taken to flight everywhere and in great haste. Papa François is not behaving very well and has withdrawn his contingent and wants to maintain it as a threat against me. Send for M. Fleuret [Floret] and say to him: "They are trying to entice my father against us. I have sent for you to ask you to write to him that the Emperor is fully prepared, he has 1 million men under arms and I foresee, if my father listens to all the Empress's prating, that he is laying up many calamities for himself. He does not know this nation, its attachment to the Emperor and its energy. Tell my father from me, as his beloved daughter, who takes such interest in him and in the land of her birth, that if my father allows himself to be overpersuaded, the French will be in Vienna before September and that he will have forfeited the friend-ship of a man who is deeply attached to him." Write to him yourself to the same effect, in his own interest more than in mine, for I have seen the way his mind has been working this long while and I am prepared. Adio, mio dolce amore.

NAP.

BOMA 5 *May*

Mon amie

I am sending you the army order; you will see that all is well. My health is very good, the weather very fine. We are in a country intersected with little hills like those at Baruth[1]. I shall be within 6 leagues of Dresden this evening. Adio, mio bene. Tout à toi.

NAP.

ERDORF 6 *May*

On May 5th the Czar and the King of Prussia had passed through Dresden; though at the time they were in precipitate retreat, they displayed such braggadocio that the inhabitants, convinced

[1] Bayreuth.

they were victorious, had greeted them with serenades. The Cossacks of the rearguard and the *baskhirs* with their quivers full of arrows had just left the city, and Miloradowitch, having burnt the bridges, had settled down at Neustadt in a suburb on the far side of the Elbe, when on the eighth of May French bayonets glittered on the horizon. Napoleon was received by a deputation at the outskirts of the city and made no secret of his displeasure. "Fragments of garlands are still clinging to your houses, and your streets are littered with a mush of the flowers your maidens strewed before the monarchs' feet. Still, I am willing to overlook all that." Under the fire of eighty guns Miloradowitch, attacked by the *voltigeurs*, beat a retreat.

Ma bonne amie

I am writing to you from Dresden. My health is very good. My affairs are in good shape. I am glad to see by your letter that the little King is well and that your health is improving. Adieu, mon amie. Tout à toi.

NAP.

VADHEIM 7 *May*

Ma bonne amie

I have received your letter of the 2nd. I hope you will have heard by yesterday the news of the victory of Lützen. My health is very good. The weather is very fine this morning. I am nearing Dresden; my outposts are within 4 leagues of it. Adieu, mio bene. Tout à toi.

NAP.

NOSSEN 8 *May*, 9 *a.m.*

Ma bonne amie

I have been in Dresden since last night. My health is very good, the weather is very fine. I fancy the battle of Lützen and my arrival at Dresden have been a great disappointment for my enemies in Vienna. Give the good news to Maman Behatris and tell her I have 1,200,000 soldiers just as good. Adieu, mon amie. Tout à toi.

NAP.

DRESDEN 9 *May*

Ma bonne amie

I have just received your letter of the 3rd. You will have received some very good news since then. I am master of both banks of the Elbe; to-morrow we are leaving in pursuit. My affairs are going well, the Russians and Prussians are deeply humiliated and soundly beaten. Adieu, mio bene. Tout à toi.

NAP.

DRESDEN 10 *May*

The victory at Lützen made the French masters of the left bank of the Elbe from Bohemia to Hamburg. Moreover, it restored to the throne Frederick Augustus, the wanderer King, who received at Prague the despatches issued from the battlefield of Lützen. He came back from Bohemia seriously perturbed as to the state of mind prevailing in the Austrian Cabinet.

153

Ma bonne amie

      I have received the King of Prussia to-day and reinstated him. My health is very good. My affairs are going well. Adio, mio bene.

NAP.

DRESDEN [12 *May*]

Write to the Vice-Reine that the Viceroy left for Milan at noon to-day.

Metternich informed the ambassador at Vienna, Narbonne-Lara, that "the alliance had changed its character, that Austria, departing from a policy of mere intervention, would now take up an attitude of 'armed mediation', and would take steps to enforce her new policy by organizing an efficient army". Meanwhile, from Dresden, whither the King of Saxony had returned with an army of a hundred thousand men, Napoleon was endeavouring to regain control of his weak-minded father-in-law.

Ma bonne amie

      I have received your letter. I am very happy to hear you are pleased with my successes. My affairs are going well. People are trying to mislead Papa François. Metternik is a mere intriguer. I have sent the Viceroy to Italy to organise my army. I shall have 100,000 men there in a month's time. Send some couriers to your father, in Vienna, through Count de la Valette. Adieu, mio bene.

NAP.

DRESDEN 14 *May*

Ma bonne amie

I have just received your letter of the 10th. It seems to me that what you have written to your father is just right. My affairs are going well. My health is good and I love you as the dearest of wives. Adio, mio bene.

NAP.

DRESDEN 15 *May, in the evening*

Ma bonne amie

I have at last received the little King's letter-case which was brought to me by Meunié. It seemed to me delightful. I thought it charming; it was a very kind attention on your part. I have had all your letters put in it. My health is very good, my affairs are going well. The Prussians who wanted to burn everything and poison everybody seem to have come back in a more chastened mood, for they published in their *Gazette*, on the 12th, that if the French Army came to Berlin, there must be no armed resistance but that they were to be received according to the customs of war. Adieu, mon amie, love me. I am told you are as fresh as spring; I should so like to be near you. Your faithful husband

NAP.

DRESDEN 16 *May*

Ma bonne amie

I have received your letter of the 11th. I read with pleasure what you have written to your father. It struck me as quite right. My health is perfect. The heat is very great. I have sent the Viceroy to Milan to organise my army against your father, who seems to be about to threaten me. I saw General Bouben[a] this evening and gave him a

155

piece of my mind. I hope they will think better of it. In any case you must not worry too much, they will be given a good drubbing. Adieu, mon amie. Love me as I love you. Tout à toi.   NAPOLEON

DR[ESDEN] 17 *May*

Mon amie
        I have seen Count Boubena, who brought me a letter from Papa François. I told him what I think about it. My health is good, my affairs are going well. I love you, as you well know. You were quite right to go to the Métropole, it will please the Parisians. Adieu, mon amie. Love me.   NAP.

DRESDEN 18 *May*

On May 17th, Napoleon wrote to the Emperor Francis: "Brother and dearly loved Father-in-Law, I have received your Majesty's letter, and I have had several hours' conversation with the Comte de Boubena. . . . No one desires peace more ardently than I. I agree to the summoning of a Congress. If, when the congress has met, the belligerent powers show a desire for the conclusion of an armistice, I am quite ready to join in it." "Like all warm-blooded Frenchmen", he added, "I would rather die, sword in hand, than yield, if an attempt be made to force conditions on me."
        Caulaincourt, on Napoleon's behalf, asked for an audience from the Czar. "My intention", the Emperor informed his delegate, "is to provide for him a 'golden bridge' which will enable his escape from Metternich's intrigues. If I have to

make sacrifices, I would rather make them for the benefit of Emperor Alexander, who is fighting a straight fight against me, and that of the King of Prussia, than for the benefit of Austria, betrayer of the alliance."

And now we come to a Virgilian eclogue on the "cherry-season" in the Montmorency valley. Is Napoleon taking a rest from battle? No, he is at war.

Mon amie   HARTHA 19 *May*

    I left Dresden yesterday at two o'clock in the afternoon. I have arrived here in a country house. My health is very good. I am surprised they did not publish your letter to the Bishops in the *Moniteur*. I hope you enjoyed yourself at St. Leu. The valley of Montmorency is very beautiful in this season, yet I fancy the time when it is pleasantest is the beginning of June when the cherries are ripe. Adio, mio bene.

                      NAP.

On a front a league and a half long, protected by the Spree, a hundred thousand Prussians and Russians—according to Napoleon's estimate, as many as a hundred and fifty thousand—had entrenched themselves between wooded mountains and fortified foothills, with trenches and redoubts to fall back on in case of need. The centre rested on the crenelated village of Bautzen. "We wish neither to advance nor to retreat", a Russian officer informed a Frenchman. The Czar and the King of Prussia watched the operations from the village of Natchen.

At noon, on May 20th, Marshals Macdonald, Oudinot and Marmont crossed the Spree on trestle bridges. General Compans occupied Bautzen, and Ney attacked the heights on which the enemy's right flank rested. At 8 p.m. Napoleon entered Bautzen, having won the day.

Mon amie

        I had a battle to-day. I took possession of Bautzen, I dispersed the Russian and Prussian armies, which had been joined by all their reinforcements and their reserves from the Vistula and held a splendid position. It was a fine battle. I am rather unwell, I got soaked 2 or 3 times during the day. I kiss you and ask you to kiss my son for me. My health is good. I lost no one of any importance, I put my losses at 3,000 men, killed and wounded. Adio, mio bene.

NAP.

BATZEN 20 *May*

On the 21st, at 5 a.m., the Emperor advanced beyond Bautzen, against the reserve entrenchments and redoubts of the Allies. While the other Marshals held the enemy's left wing closely engaged, Ney crossed the Spree, and outflanking the opposing forces, advanced in the direction of Wurschen. The Czar and the King of Prussia, now that their right wing was turned, began a retreat, which rapidly degenerated into a headlong flight.

The battle had lasted thirty-four hours. During the whole period the Emperor took no rest. On the second day, utterly worn out, he dismounted and lay down near a ravine, on a slope occupied by Marmont's batteries; despite the ear-racking din he fell asleep. Caulaincourt awoke him with the news that the battle had been won. "Which confirms the saying", the Emperor observed as he sprang on to his horse, "that good things come to him who sleeps."

* * *

On May 22nd, at 7 p.m., Napoleon gallops off towards a hill overlooking Nieder-Markersdorf, where the fighting has not yet come to an end. Mortier, Caulaincourt, Duroc and Kirgener follow him. "My field-glass, my field-glass", he says. Caulaincourt turns round: the two of them are alone. A stray cannon-ball has killed Kirgener and disembowelled Duroc. Duroc, Grand Marshal and Duke of Friuli, who combined the highest qualities of a private individual with the virtues of a great citizen! Napoleon bends over the dying man, who presses his hand and carries it to his lips.

And here I will quote the *Bulletin de la Grande Armée*: "All my life has been devoted to your service, and I regret it only on account of any further use it might have been to you." "Duroc", said the Emperor, "there is another life. There you will await my coming." "Yes, Sire, when you have fulfilled all the hopes of our fatherland. I have lived worthily, I have nothing to blame myself for. I leave a daughter. Your Majesty will be a father to her." And after a long silence:

"Ah! Sire, leave me; the sight of me is painful to you." "Adieu, then, my friend!" And leaning on the Duc de Dalmatie and the Grand Equerry, Napoleon went back in silence to his tent.

Ma bonne amie

 I have received your letter. You will have heard of the fateful cannon-ball which killed the Grand Marshal (Duroc) and General Kirgener. Fancy my grief; you know how fond I was of the Duc de Frioul. My affairs are going very well. The enemy is being followed up actively and is nowhere making a stand, as you will see in the news. Adio mio bene. Tout à toi.

NAP.

IN CAMP NEAR GÖRLITZ, *the* 23*rd*, 9 *a.m.*

Provisionally, the duties of Grand Marshal were carried out by the Grand Equerry, Caulaincourt.

Ma bonne amie

 I was very sad all day yesterday over the death of the Duc de Frioul. He was a friend of twenty years' standing. Never did I have any occasion to complain of him, he was never anything but a comfort to me. He is an irreparable loss, the greatest I could suffer in the Army. I have ordered the Master of the Horse to discharge his duties until I appoint some one to replace him. Adio, mio bene. My affairs are going very well. Tout à toi.

NAP.

GORLITZ, 24 *May*

CAULAINCOURT
(Armand Augustin Louis, Marquis de Caulaincourt,
Duke of Vicenza, Master of the Horse, 1773-1827.)

DUROC
(Géraud Christophe Michel Duroc, Duke of Friuli,
Grand Marshal 1772-1813)

"Madame et chère Amie", he wrote officially to the Empress Regent, "I beg you to speak to the Archchancellor and to the Minister of War, so that they may instruct the best of our young orators to pronounce the funeral orations of the Dukes of Istria and Friuli."

He informs the Emperor Francis of his victory: "Monsieur mon Frère et très cher Beau-Père, I gave battle on the 20th and 21st to the Russian and Prussian Army, entrenched at the camps of Bautzen and Hochkirch. Providence granted me the victory."

And in order to weigh more heavily on the decision of the Vienna Cabinet, he informs the daughter of the Emperor Francis that Prince Eugène de Beauharnais is building up a big army in Italy.

Mon amie

I have just received your letter of the 19th. I am very glad of what you write about the state of your health and that of my son, who, I presume, has grown considerably and is now a fluent speaker. Order a fine portrait of him. You will have been given particulars of the battle by Montesquiou. My affairs are going well. My health is very good. I hope the battle of Vurzen will moderate the ambition of the Vienna cabinet. To meet contingencies, I have assembled an army of 120,000 men in Italy, that is what I sent the Viceroy there for. Adieu, mon amie, my health is very good. Tout à toi.

NAP.

25 May

From Görlitz, Oudinot inclines towards Berlin, in pursuit of Bülow, Ney towards Bunzlau, Hainau, Liegnitz and Glogau, at the heels of Barclay and Yorck. Napoleon appears to make out that all is well in his letters to the Arch-chancellor Cambacérès and to Marie-Louise.

"We are in the heart of Silesia", he writes to the former. "We are pressing on in pursuit of the enemy. The alarm about Austria is taken far too seriously in Paris."

And to the latter:

Mon amie
        I have received your letter of the 15th. As you see, my affairs are going well. My health is very good; I long to hear that you were pleased with the ceremony of the Te Deum. You know how I love you. I wish it was all over and I could see you again. Adio, mio bene. Tout à toi.

                            NAP.

26 *May* IN THE SMALL TOWN OF BRUZELM, IN SÉLÉSIE [SILESIA]

Mon amie
        I was concerned to read in your letter of the 22nd that you were feeling unwell. I hope that on the 23rd you will have been in good spirits and that you will have borne up well under the fatigue of the ceremony. My health is good; my affairs are going well. Adieu, mon amie. Tout à toi.

                            NAP.

29 *May*

Mon amie

I have received your letter of May 23rd. I am very sorry you did not reprieve the man condemned to death before going to the Te Deum. Such an act of mercy would have been appropriate on a day of rejoicing; the Archchancellor has been over-stern in this matter. I love you as much as you deserve, or in other words, as much as possible. Adio, mio bene. Tout à toi.

NAP.

FROM THE FARM OF ROGLIN (?) 30 *May*

Mon amie

I have just received your letter of the 25th. You have been informed of the battle of Vurzen, which will have made you easier in your mind. My health is good, my affairs are going well. My troops have doubtless entered Breslau this evening. Adio, mio bene. Your faithful husband

NAP.

NEUMARCK 31 *May*

Ma bonne amie

I have just received your letter of May 28th. It was childish of you to suppose that any one could have objected to your not receiving on account of ill-health. Everybody will have thought that quite natural. Those who reported such remarks to you are silly fools. My health is good, be careful of yours. Give two kisses to my son and never doubt your [faithful] husband

NAP.

[*undated*]

163

Ma bonne amie

      I have received your letter of the 28th, by which I see that you are very distressed. I hope the news of a two months' armistice that will have reached you by the telegraph from Mayence will have given you pleasure. My affairs are going well. My health is good. Be careful of yours. Give my son two kisses on the eyes and love your faithful husband well.

NAP.

NEUMARCK 4 *June*

I shall proceed to Dresden during the armistice, so as to be nearer to you.

Hard pressed, Generals Shuvalov and Kleist presented themselves at the outposts under a flag of truce. And on June 4th a two months' armistice was signed at Plaeswitz between France, Russia and Prussia. "Austria still made a show of playing the part of peacemaker", declared Caulaincourt, "but the pact with France was torn up, and we knew it. The armistice was a misfortune." Napoleon, after his victory, moved back to Dresden, just as though he had been defeated.

Ma chère amie

      I am going to Hanau this evening, and by the time you read this, I shall be in Dresden. So you see I am coming nearer to you. My health is good, my affairs are in very good shape. I love you and long to see you. A kiss to my son, and never doubt your [husband].

NAP.

LIGNITZ 6 *June*

Ma bonne amie

I have received your letter of July 1st. I was sorry to hear you did not enjoy yourself at the Council of State. It is not a bad thing that you should preside over it once every month. I shall be at Dresden on the 9th, the day after to-morrow. You will certainly have heard that we entered Hambour. I hope you ordered our squadrons to be dressed and salutes to be fired for the battle of Vurzen. My health is very good. I love you and long to see you. A kiss, please, to my son. Adio, mio bene. Tout à toi.

NAP.

BRUNZELAU, 7 *June*

Mon amie

I shall be in Dresden to-night, in good health, yet the weather has been very hot to-day. I was in the saddle all day long. Give a kiss to my son; all you tell me about him makes me long to see him, but it is you, mon amie, whom I should particularly like to kiss. Adio, mio bene.

NAP.

BAUZEN, 9*th*, 7 *p.m.*

Ma bonne amie

I have reached Dresden at 4 o'clock in the morning. I have taken up my quarters in a small suburban house belonging to Count Marcelin, standing in very fine grounds, which is very pleasant for me. You know how dreary the King's palace is. My health is very good. Give a kiss to my son. You know how I love you.

NAP.

DRESDEN 10 *June*, 1 *p.m.*

Mon amie

I am dining to-day at the King of Saxony's where I shall meet your aunt Thérèse. The heat is beginning to be very great. I was in the saddle yesterday from twelve to four. I came back with a touch of sunstroke. My health is very good. I hope you will have enjoyed yourself at Mortfontaine, roaming through the fine lakes and the park which is well laid out. You must give presents to those of the officers of the Queen of Spain and of Hortense who have served you. There is nothing new. Adio, mio bene. Tout à toi.

Your faithful

DRESDEN 13 *June* NAP.

On June 13th, he received the King of Saxony and his brothers, who had come to pay their respects to him in uniform; after he attended church and sang a *Te Deum*. The midday meal was partaken of at the palace of King Frederick Augustus. The Aunt Thérèse, referred to several times in the letters to the Empress, from whom she complained of not having heard, was Marie-Thérèse of Austria, daughter of the Emperor Leopold II and wife of Prince Antoine de Saxe.

Ma bonne amie

I have received your letter of June 10th. I am sorry you had bad weather at Mortfontaine. You would have enjoyed going on the water. What you tell me of my son makes me very anxious to see him. I read in the *Moniteur* that you announced the Te Deum and your presence in the Métropole, I hope

166

therefore, that you went there; you should never countermand such functions. My health is good, the weather is very hot here, there is a storm every day. Give two kisses to my son and never doubt all the sentiments of your f[aithful husband].   NAP.

DRESDEN 16 *June*

Mortfontaine, in the Oise Department, at a distance of ten kilometres from Senlis, was one of the finest landscape gardens in Europe, and belonged to Joseph Bonaparte. A small and a large park, an archipelago of islets in a lake, sheer rocks, an orangery and an aviary, rendered it an enchanting spot.

But what call was there, with so many pleasing classical remembrances—Grotto of the Naiads, Grotto of the Cupids, Altar to the Rural Divinities, Modest Venus, Philemon and Baucis—for the addition of funeral monuments reminiscent of the end of all things here below: tombs, a cenotaph and tear-bespangled sarcophagus? It was at Mortfontaine that a rural fête was given on September 30th, 1800, on the occasion of a Treaty of Peace with the United States.

Ma bonne amie

I was glad to hear you were in good health; you must take great care of yourself and not go out in the damp, that is the cause of the pains you feel in your chest. I have had little Italian plays the last two days but the singers are very bad. My health is good. Give a kiss to my son. Tout à toi.   NAP.

DRESDEN 21 *June*

The Italian plays attended by Napoleon in a small playhouse set up in the Palace Orangery, were *Il Corradino*, an opera by Kapelmeister Morlacchi, and *La Stella della Sposa*.

Ma bonne amie

I have received your letter. Poor Madame de Broc's adventure is a very sad one. I had the whole Saxony family to dinner to-day. Your aunt Thérèse complains that you no longer write to her. My health is very good. I love you with all my heart.

A kiss to my son. NAP.

22 *June*

After dinner, Napoleon treated his guests to a performance of *La Gageure* and *La suite d'un bal masqué*. His brother Jerome, King of Westphalia, had joined him. Napoleon had just attended the performance of *Tartuffe*, when by a strange coincidence Metternich was announced.

Ma bonne amie   DRESDEN 24 [*June*]

I have received your letter. I was glad to hear you enjoyed yourself at Maison, but it is a pity the weather was bad. I am dining with the King, to-day, after which I shall attend a performance of *Le Tartufe*. My health is very good. The King of Westphalia is here. My affairs are going well and I am pleased at all you tell me about my son; I long to see him. Give him a kiss from me. I should much like you to be here, but it is not suitable. Adio, mio bene. Ton

NAP.

Mon amie

I have been for an excursion of about twenty leagues, to-day, in the woods round Dresden. I got back at 10 o'clock at night. My health is very good. Meternic arrived at Dresden this afternoon. We shall see what he has to say and what Papa François wants. He is still adding to his army in Bohemia; I am strengthening mine in Italy. Give a kiss to your son; I long to see him. Adio, mio bene.

NAP.

DRESDEN 25 *June*

Ma bonne amie

I had a long and wearisome talk with Metternich. My health is good, however. What you tell me of the little King's jealous disposition made me laugh. I should so like to see him. Give him 3 kisses from me. Have you seen the elephant at the Jardin des Plantes? I hope that peace will be negotiated in a few days' time. I want peace, but it must be an honorable one. Adio, mio bene. Tout à toi.

NAP.

DRESDEN 27 *June*

Napoleon goes into no particulars as to the fatiguing conversation he has had with Metternich. Metternich, on the contrary, has recorded it in his *Memoirs*. On his arrival at the estate of Marcolini, Grand Equerry of the King of Saxony, he was shown into the Emperor's study.

"It depends on Your Majesty to give peace to the world and to base his rule on a feeling of universal gratitude. If Your Majesty allows this opportunity to escape, to what lengths may not the extent of the upheaval go?"

"I am prepared to make peace, but not a dishonourable peace. I have written to that effect to the Emperor [of Austria]. My honour first, then peace. Do you mean to strip me? Do you want Italy, Brabant, Lorraine? I will not yield an inch of territory. I will make peace on the basis of the *status quo ante*."

Ma bonne amie

I received your letter this morning; I am glad to see your health is good. Your aunt Thérèse complains that you do not write to her. I went for a several hours' outing yesterday. My health is good. Adio, mio amor.

NAP.

DRESDEN 29 *June*

In the evening, for the sake of diversion, he attends a performance of *La Jeunesse d'Henri V, roi d'Angleterre*.

On June 30th, at half-past two, Napoleon sent for Metternich. He had with him a four hours' conference, the character of which is revealed in the following letter:

Mon amie

I have received your letter; all you tell me of your sentiments gives me pleasure. My health is very good. They tell me the little King is a little wretch. I should much like to see him even for a day,

170

METTERNICH
(Clemens Wenzel Lothar, Count of Metternich-Winneburg,
1773-1859.)

A portrait by Gudin.

THE EMPRESS MARIE-LOUISE

but I am afraid it is not yet possible. I think the peace conferences will begin before July 5th, at Prague. Metternich, whom I have seen, strikes me as an intriguer and as directing Papa François very badly. The man has not enough sense for his position. Mille choses aimables.

NAP.

DRESDEN 1 *July*

A kind attention of Marie-Louise, whom he is hoping to meet again shortly, and who has sent him some engravings, enables him to make a present to her aunt Marie-Thérèse, who is constantly complaining of her niece's silence. He gives his wife a further lesson in propriety: she is to request her lady-in-waiting, the Duchesse de Montebello, the widow of the late General Lannes, no longer to issue invitations indiscriminately.

Ma bonne amie

I have received your letter of the 23rd and the beautiful engraving that accompanied it; it is very good of you, but I assure you I have no need of this to think very often of ma bonne Louise. I should love to see her; let us hope I shall before long. I confess to having given your engraving to aunt Thérèse, who complains of you and who was much pleased with it. Pray send me another. Tell me by whom it is. Have him informed that I thought it very beautiful. Adio mio bene.

NAP.

[DRESDEN, *undated*]

Mon amie

I am answering your letter of June 27th. I have sent the Duc de Dalmatie to Spain to take command in lieu of the King, who is no soldier

171

and knows nothing about anything. The Duchess
manages her invitations very badly and it has a very
bad effect. For instance, she will ask people who
have been away from Paris for a month, or even for 3,
which makes people laugh and leads them to think
this work of sending out invitations is done by a clerk,
the result being that they are no longer flattered at
being asked. See to this. Draw up your list yourself, for the dear Duchess is not good for much.
General Cafarelly should send in a list of the officers
and prefects who are in Paris, so as to avoid asking
people who are away. Adio, mio bene. Give three
kisses to the little King.

Ton   NAP.

DRESDEN 2 *July*

King of Spain and the Indies, Joseph Bonaparte was held in subjection by the Emperor, who
had sent a French General to take command at
Madrid, and placed Spain under the supervision
of the French Police. On leaving for Russia,
however, Napoleon had restored his brother to
the supreme command of the armies in Spain.
But Joseph met with nothing but reverses. While
falling back from Madrid to Valladolid, then to
Vittoria, he was attacked in the latter place, on
June 21st, 1813, by Wellington, who picked up a
great many prisoners and captured one hundred
and fifty guns, as well as the coach containing the
King's correspondence.

Ma bonne Louise

     I am very sorry to hear your health is not as
good as it should be. Pray take care of yourself and
keep well. You know how dear you are to me. Your

aunt Thérèse complains of your laziness. My health
is very good. Give two kisses to my son. I long to
see him, after all you tell me about him. He must
have grown a good deal in the last 3 months. Adio,
mio bene. I love you. Tout à toi.

NAP.

DRESDEN 5 *July*

Napoleon attends a performance of *Les Fausses
Confidences* and *Le Barbier de Séville*. But the
time to take weighty decisions is at hand. On
hearing of the reverses to his brother Joseph,
he issues a decree placing the armies of
Spain and Portugal under the sole command of
Marshal Soult, Duc de Dalmatie, with Reille,
Clausel, d'Erlon and Guzan as seconds. King
Joseph made over the high command to Soult on
July 12th. And knowing full well that Joseph
will again take up his residence in his beautiful
estate of Mortfontaine, he dictates a line of
conduct to Marie-Louise.

Ma bonne Louise
　　　　I have received your letter of July 2nd. I
was anxious about your health, so I am glad to hear
you are well again. I am sending the Duc de Dalmatie
to Spain; the King knows nothing about it, and not
only is he no soldier, but he manages badly. If he
comes to Marfontaine, it must be *incognito* and you
must ignore him; I will not have him interfere with
the government, or intrigues set up in Paris. Inform
the Archchancellor that you agree that he shall tell
you how to act. My health is very good. Peace
would be made if Austria were not trying to fish in

troubled waters. The Emperor is deceived by Metternich, who has been bribed by the Russians; he is a man, moreover, who believes that politics consist in telling lies. I think the Congress will meet in 2 days' time. We shall see what is done there. If they attempt to impose shameful terms upon me, I will make war upon them. Austria will pay for it all. I should be sorry for this on account of the grief it would give you, but one cannot put up with injustice. The English have landed your grandmother at Constantinople, whence she will proceed to Buda. Adio, mio bene. Tout à toi.

NAP.

DRESDEN 7 *July*

Ma bonne amie

Thank you for your beautiful engravings. I have made a present of them and they have given much pleasure. My health is very good: I am going to Vittenberg to-morrow, 30 leagues from here, to view some troops and fortifications. I beg you to keep well and never doubt

ton NAP.

DR[ESDEN] 9 *July*

I have received your letter of July 6th, ma bonne amie, and I am answering it from Wittenberg. I spent all day visiting the fortifications and viewing the 5th and 6th Divisions; it was rather tiring on account of the great heat. Otherwise my health is very good. I am going to spend the night at Desseau, where I have 10,000 [men] to view. To-morrow, I shall proceed to Magdeb[urg], and on the 14th I shall be at Dresden. Give a kiss to my son and never doubt

NAP.

VITTENBERG 11 *July*

Ma bonne amie

      I have received your letter of July 7th. I was sorry to hear you were fretting and that what I wrote to you about the Duchess had grieved you. I have come here to see my troops and the town, which is one of the strongest places in the world. I am very satisfied with them. I have had news of myself conveyed to you by the telegraph. I had news of you yesterday, which reached me in 42 hours. Kiss my son and never doubt all my sentiments. Tout à toi.

NAP.

MAGDEBOURG 12 *July*

Ma bonne amie

      I have received your letter of the 8th. I am leaving presently, so as to be at Dresden on the 14th. I shall see some troops at Leipsik on my way. The heat is very great, which makes travelling rather painful. My health, however, is very good. Give a kiss to the little King and never doubt the sentiments I [bear you].

NAP.

MAGDEBOURG 13 *July*

Briefly, the Emperor reviewed the 5th, 6th and 6th-b Divisions at Wittemberg; the Philippon Division at Dessang; the three Divisions under Vandamme at Magdeburg; the Duc de Padoue's three Divisions at Leipzig; the Saxon troops at Dresden. Well may he rest him of his "trip".

Ma bonne Louise

I got back this morning from my rounds. The weather is still very sultry. I was very satisfied with the Equerry Lambertini—you can take him, he is a very good servant. Adieu, mio bene. Tout à toi.

NAP.

DRESDEN 15 *July*

To the Prague Conferences, whence peace or war were to emerge, he has deputed his Grand Equerry, Caulaincourt, and his Ambassador at Vienna, Count Louis de Narbonne-Lara, a diplomat of the old school, with fine manners and a pleasantly ironical address, but flighty, "the type of the brilliant butterflies of the panniers age in the reign of Louis XV", as Napoleon called him.

Ma bonne Louise

I have received your letter of July 11th. I believe that the conferences in Prague will at last begin in 2 or three days' time. I reckon sending the Duc de Vicence and the Comte de Narbonne. Meanwhile my armies in Italy and Bavaria are being organized, and if we are to fight, your father would be very unwise to let himself be drawn into it. He would make his countries the theatre of war. Write to your father to that effect. My health is very good. Adio, mio bene. Tout à toi.

NAP.

DRESDEN 16 *July*

During the conferences at Prague, Napoleon summoned the Empress to Mayence, no doubt with a view to consulting with her as to a final appeal to "Papa François".

Mon amie

I want to see you. You will set out on the 22nd, spend the night at Châlons; be at Metz on the 23rd, and on the 24th at Mayance, where I shall join you. You will travel with 4 coaches in the 1st train, 4 coaches in the second, 4 in the 3rd. You will take with you the Duchess, 2 ladies-in-waiting, a prefect of the Palace, 2 Chamberlains, 2 pages, a physician and 2 red ladies, 2 black ladies and your dinner service. Have a coach to yourself. See to all this. The Comte Cafarelli will be in command of the escorts and lead the way. Inform the Archchancellor of all this. Adieu, mon amie. There will be time for you to hear from me again before you leave. Tout à toi.

NAP.

DRESDEN 16 *July*

The "red" ladies and "black" ladies are neither Indian women, nor negresses. The colour of their dresses is responsible for these designations. On receiving this letter, Marie-Louise is overjoyed, for it is three months since she saw her husband last. She determines to travel day and night. But no sooner has she reached Châlons, than she realizes how necessary is sleep. Drums and tambourines, with their appalling din, keep her awake till one o'clock in the morning, she tells us in her Diary.

Ma bonne amie

I wrote to you yesterday, I hope my letter will have given you pleasure. My health is very good. The weather is very hot. Pray keep me informed as

M 177

to your journey and believe in the happiness it gives me to think I shall be seeing you soon. Adio, mio bene.

NAP.

DRESDEN 17 *July*

The following letter is one of the most charming ever written by Napoleon. Can it have derived its inspiration from the plays he had attended that day at the Dresden playhouse: *Les Epreuves nouvelles* and *Les Secrets du Ménage?*

Ma bonne amie

I have received your letter of the 13th. I am glad to hear the ceremony at Notre-Dame went off well. You must not be put out by what I write to you, because it is to train you, and in view of the future, for you know I am very pleased with you and that even were you to do something that was not to my liking, I should think it quite natural; you can never do anything that would make me angry, you are too good and too perfect for that. But I shall continue when I see something that I do not agree with, to tell you so, without your feeling aggrieved thereby. I have given orders that when a mass has been ordered, or a play, it is not to be countermanded. They can both be performed without either of us being present, if we wish not to attend them, but in that case there would be no objection. When the play was to have taken place within doors, the guests should be admitted just the same to the apartments intended for the purpose, and there the following announcement should be made to them: "Their Majesties will not attend the performance; there will be none, but every one is to remain as long as they please in the apartments," and so there is no evil effect. When the performance is to take place in the playhouse, it should be pro-

178

ceeded with, whether either of us is present or not. Explain this to Cafarelly and the Grand Chamberlain and the Duchess. Adio, mio bene. Tout à toi.

NAP.

A kiss to my son.

DRESDEN 18 *July*

Ma bonne Louise

To-morrow I shall go on a 100 miles round in Lusatia, I shall be back on the 22nd, and shall leave on the 23rd for Mayence, which I shall reach in 40 hours' time. My health is very good and I am looking forward with great pleasure to seeing you again. Adio, mio bene.

NAP.

DRESDEN 19 *July*

Mon amie

I was to have left this morning at six, but affairs prevented me from doing so. I am leaving at midday for Lusatia. My health is good. It is raining hard. I presume you will receive this letter at Châlons. It will give me a great happiness to send it off and to have you with me for a few days. Adieu, mon amie. A loving kiss.

NAP.

DRESDEN 20 *July*

It was at Luckau, Luben and Gaben that Napoleon was about to hold reviews.

Ma bonne amie

I was to have set out this afternoon, but I shall only be doing so in the night of the 24th. I have some affairs that will keep me here for another 24 hours. You may imagine how annoyed I am, for I presume you will be at Mayence on the 24th. Adieu, ma douce amie. Tout à toi.

NAP.

DRESDEN 23 *July*

179

By the letter delivered to her by General Fouler, Marie-Louise hears that Napoleon will be at Mayence on the 27th. She gets there before him, and from the house at which she had put up the previous year, she gazes once more at the beautiful Rhine scenery, in the direction of the pontoon bridge—the Wiesbaden and Malibocus hills, crowned by a Roman Tower. The Prefect "Jambon" (Jean Bon) Saint-André comes and pays his respects to her. The Emperor is inspecting the fortifications at Cassel. She joins him there and they both proceed along the Rhine together, like plain commoners, as far as Mayence, where the Emperor requests of her, on the 28th, after dinner, the favour of a drive.

Ma bonne Louise

I was very sad all night long; I had already grown accustomed to being with you, it is so sweet! And I felt very lonely. Let us hope that before a month has passed we shall be together for a long time. I arrived at the Prince Primat's at half past eleven. I expect to be at Vürzb[urg] early to-morrow. Adieu, ma bonne amie; love me and take great care of yourself. Your faithful husband NAP.

VURSBURG I *Aug.*

Napoleon left Mayence at five o'clock in the afternoon to return to Dresden. Sending his secretary, Baron Fain, on ahead, he reviews two Bavarian Divisions at Zelle, near Magdeburg; two Divisions of the Bavarian observation army at Bamberg; the French and Bavarian troops at Bayreuth, on August 3rd; and the Dupar Division at Hof.

Ma bonne amie
        2 a.m. on the 5th

  I reached Dresden on the 4th at 6 o'clock in the morning. I stopped at Vürsburg, at Bamberg, at Bareuth,[1] to see some troops, and yet I was but three hours behind Fain. I have not yet received the estafette of June 1st, but I have just received a courier whom Ménevalle sent to me with the telegraphic dispatch of June 1st, afternoon. My health is very good. I have been thinking of you very often and I very much wish to see you and never to leave you again. I am writing to the Archchancellor and the Minister of Marine (to enquire) whether the works can be postponed, it would be a very good thing for you to go to Cherbourg to enjoy that fine sight. NAP.

Ma chère Louise

  I have received your letter from Coblentz. I am sorry to hear you were incommoded by the noise; I hope this letter will find you in Paris, in good health. Give two kisses to my son. Have a good rest before going to Cherbourg, the sight will be a very fine one, you will enjoy it. Adio, mio bene. NAP.

DR[ESDEN] 6 *Aug.*

Ma bonne amie

  The Army celebrated my Saint's Day, to-day, I had a very fine parade of 40,000 men. The King and the Prince of Saxony attended it. This evening, I am going to the Court banquet and afterwards to the display of fireworks. The weather is fine, fortunately. My health is very good. I suppose you will leave for Cherbourg on the 17th. I wish you much enjoyment. You will tell me what you have seen. Adieu, mon amie. Tout à toi. NAP.

DRESDEN 10 *Aug.*

   [1] Bayreuth.

At the extremity of the Cotentin peninsula, reaching far out into the Channel, the important situation of Cherbourg had escaped the observation neither of Vauban, who had started defensive works there, which were suspended by Louvois, nor of Louis XVI, who drew up the map of the place with his own hand. For the opening of the Cherbourg dock, the arrival of the Empress was awaited.

On August 9th, Napoleon attended a performance of *Cinna*. Owing to the uncertainty of the political developments, public rejoicings were held at Dresden, on the morrow, five days before his Saint's Day. To these reference is made in his letter of the 11th.

Mon amie

I have received your letter of August 8th, from Namur. My health is very good. I hope you will not have been fatigued by the journey, and that you will have found the little King much grown; tell me if he recognized you. Kiss him three times for me. The weather has turned fine since yesterday. The show yesterday went off very well and was very gay both for the men and for the people. Adio, mio bene. Tout à toi.

NAP.

DRESDEN 11 *Aug.*

And amid his anxiety about the immediate future, how he envies Marie-Louise, to whom it is given to attend the magnificent sight of the opening of the Cherbourg dock and to visit the largest province in France, the one that gives him his best sailors—Brittany!

Ma bonne amie

I trust you will set out for Cherbourg on the
17th. Do not tire yourself but travel by easy stages.
You know how dear to me you are and how precious
your health is to me. Write to me in detail. My health
is good, the weather is very fine, the heat has set in again.
Adio, mio bene; two kisses to my son. Tout à toi. NAP.

DRESDEN 12 *Aug.*

Mon amie

I presume you are on your way to Cherbourg. You will like the Normands, I hope, and
Cherbourg—a very fine sight which I envy you; write to
me in detail. My health is very good and I beg you never
to doubt all my sentiments. Your Faithful husband

DRESDEN 14 *Aug.*   NAP.

Caulaincourt returned from Prague—where
he had been sent to see the Emperor of Austria
on "family business"—on being informed of the
imminent declaration of war against France.
Amid the general conflagration, "Papa François",
a man of a kindly disposition, but timorous withal,
and lacking in resolution, had not the courage to
face the consequences the family pact might entail
for his country. "See Metternich", he says.

Of the result of the conversations he had held
with the Austrian Minister, Caulaincourt apprizes
Napoleon:

"Well, Caulaincourt?"

"I believe, sire, that Austria will side with
Prussia and Russia."

"That is your opinion, but it is not a fact. On
what do you base that opinion?"

"The last day but one before the date fixed for the breaking of the armistice, Blücher marched into Silesia at the head of one hundred thousand men and captured Breslau. That very same day Jomini deserted from Marshal Ney's staff, and he is now with the Emperor Alexander. Sweden, too, is moving against us . . ."

"Nonsense! . . . Bernadotte, Bernadotte, moving against France! . . ."

"Yes, indeed, Bernadotte. And not to have to bear his brothers' curses alone, he has won over General Moreau."

Ma bonne amie

I have received your letter of the . . . (gap). I have read what your father writes to you. It is he who wanted war, through ambition and unbounded greed. Events will decide the matter. My health is very good, take care of yourself and give two kisses to the little King. Adieu, mio bene. Tout à toi.

DRESDEN 15 *Aug.* NAP.

Ma bonne amie

I have received your letter in which I read that you will set out for Cherbourg on the 19th, so this letter will not reach you in Paris. I thank you for the present you intend to give me. I cannot imagine what it will be. Choose what suits you for the journey. There is no objection to your passing through Rennes, it is the capital of Brittany, the largest province in France. You should stop at least 3 days in that town, on your way. Brest is in that province. Our best sailors are Bretons. I am at Bautzen. My health is very good and I beg you to keep well. Tout à toi. Your faithful husband NAP.

DRESDEN 16 *Aug.*

X

THE CAMPAIGN IN GERMANY

THE SUMMER AND AUTUMN CAMPAIGN—
THE DEFEAT

THE Allied nations had denounced the Armistice on August 11th, at noon, and given notice that hostilities would be renewed on the 17th, at midnight. "Papa François" had now sided with them and henceforth, in his letters, Napoleon only calls him "ton père", except when he refers to him ironically.

The Army Order sent to the Empress on August 20th announces the constitution of a large enemy army in Bohemia. Here the pick of the Russian and Prussian troops, under Barclay de Tolly, Wittgenstein and Miloradowitch have joined the Austrian forces under Schwarzenberg. A Prussian army is gathering in Silesia under Blücher and Yorck. Prussian and Swedish Corps are covering Berlin. Half a million men, with huge reserves, are preparing to cut off Napoleon in Saxony—where he has but half that number of troops.

To impede the concentration of his enemies at Prague, and to obtain a reliable notion as to their plans, Napoleon moves to Zittau, forces the passes leading out of Bohemia, crosses the mountain-chain dividing Bohemia from Lausitz and marches into Gabel. He is soon within eighteen leagues of Prague, having driven before him a general who eventually took fearful revenge on him—Neipperg:

Mon amie

I am off this evening to Goerlitz. War has been declared. Deceived by Metternich, your father has sided with my enemies. The Emperor Alexander arrived at Prague, on the 15th, the Russians are in Bohemia. My health is very good. I want you to be brave and to keep well. Adio, mio dolce amore. Tout à toi.

DRESDEN 17 *Aug.*   NAP.

Ma bonne Louise

I am writing to you from Rosenb[ach]; I shall be at Görlitz this evening. I hope you are well and that you are pleased with Cherbourg. Do not worry too much about your father's conduct; he has been misled, as he has been before sometimes. Never doubt all the sentiments I bear you. Tout à toi.

REICHEN[BACH] 18 *Aug.*   NAP.

Ma bonne Louise

I went to Bohemia yesterday. I drove out General Néperg. The Russians and Prussians have entered Bohemia. I am on my way to Lowenberg. My affairs are taking on a favourable appearance. My health is very good. You are leaving to-day for Cherbourg. Tout à toi.

ZEVITTAU [ZITTAU] 20 *Aug.*   NAP.

Now there came a sudden change of front. Napoleon moved against the Prussian forces on their way from Silesia, and by the actions at Goldberg and Bunzlau compelled Blücher to fall back, on August 23rd, behind the Katsbach. He was about to press on in pursuit, when he heard that Dresden was threatened by Schwarzenberg, debouching from Bohemia with the main army of the Allied nations.

Ma bonne amie

Hostilities have begun. I have beaten one of the enemy armies in several fights and compelled him to retreat. I have entered Bohemia and approached to within 12 leagues from Prague. One of my armies will be at Berlin to-day. I am marching on Dresden to attack a Russian and Austrian army which is debouching[1] in that direction. My affairs are going well, my health is excellent. I love you with all . . . (gap). Adieu, mon amie. Tout à toi.

NAP.

GORLITZ 24 *Aug.*

Ma bonne amie

I have received your letter from Cherbourg; it gave me much pleasure. I was delighted with what you tell me of the loyalty of my people in Normandy and the beauty of the dock. My health is good, my affairs are going well. You [will] find enclosed an order on La Boullerie for 50,000 livres. Adio, mio bene.

NAP.

1 *Sept.*

[1] The word *débouche* is written over *passe*.

Ma chère amie

    I have received your letter from Cherbourg, and I see you were pleased with the dock; it is really a fine sight, unique in its way. I should have been very happy to make the journey in your company. I hope you are back, in good health. Give two kisses to the little King, on my behalf. They tell me he speaks like an orator. I am curious to see it. The heat has begun slightly. Affairs are in pretty fair shape. My health is very good. Adieu, mio bene. Tout à toi.

NAP.

The Russians have burned more than 10 villages or small towns in Bohemia. This is not likely to please Papa François.

Among dangers of all kinds in the midst of battle, the repeated references to Cherbourg in Napoleon's correspondence bear witness to the importance he attaches to this advanced naval base—a gun pointed at the heart of England. The particulars requested of the Empress and duly sent by her, we are able to supply, failing the actual letters of Marie-Louise, from the writings of Méneval, to whom she related her journey.

Dead beat and aching all over on account of the bad conditions of the roads followed beyond Carentan, Marie-Louise repairs to the harbour, where the dock is to be formally opened on her Saint's Day, August 25th. Attended by the Minister of Marine, she visited it in its dry state, previous to the destruction of the dam, near

which a graceful stand had been set up to receive
her. After the sailors of the Guard had effected
sundry openings in the dam, the Bishop of
Coutances recited the customary prayers and
blessings, just as the sea water rushed into the
dock: the scene is depicted in a sepia drawing
by Bourgeois, preserved at the Louvre, in the
Musée de la Marine.

Schwarzenberg marched on the capital of
Saxony with 200,000 Austro-Russians and Prussians. Gouvion Saint-Cyr had but 17,000 men
with whom to oppose them. At 4 p.m., on
August 26th, six dense columns came down from
the hills round Dresden. The Russians and
Prussians were soon in possession of the suburb of
Pirna, when, to their amazement, the gates of the
city swing open and four Divisions of the Young
Guard emerge at the double, led by Ney. Murat
attacks the assailants on their left flank, Mortier
on their right. Though the enemy was unaware
of it, Napoleon had entered Dresden that very
same morning, amid the cheers of the population.
Their (the enemy's) artillery was carried at the
double.

On August 27th, Napoleon took the offensive
under pouring rain. In the centre, a lively
cannonade holds Schwarzenberg's attention, while
Murat, with his gold-embroidered cloak back
over his shoulder and a plume in his headdress,
sabres the left wing of the enemy, which is being
crushed by Marshal Victor. Cut off from the
Austrian Army, Klonau lays down his arms. It
is reported that some high personage has had an

amputation and has bled to death. Wandering on the field of battle, a greyhound is picked up with the words: "I belong to General Moreau" engraved on his collar. The doubt is solved. By a stroke of poetic justice, the traitor has had both legs cut off by a French cannon-ball.

Mon amie

I have just gained a great victory at Dresden over the Austrian, Russian and Prussian armies under the 3 sovereigns in person. I am riding off in pursuit. My health is good. One of my orderly officers Bérenger was mortally wounded. Have the news conveyed to his family and to his young wife. Adieu, mio bene. I am sending you some flags.   NAP.

[*undated*—27 *Aug.* DRESDEN]

Ma bonne amie

You will see the news in the bulletins. Papa François has had the good sense not to come along. Emperor Alexander and the King of Prussia were with the colours; they fought very well and retired in all haste. My health is very good. Adieu, mio bene.   NAP.

I expect to have a letter from you to-morrow from Prague.

[*undated*] [1813, 28 *Aug.* DRESDEN]

Mon amie

I have had some fine battles. I have given Prince Schwarzenberg and Emperor Alexander a good trouncing. The troops of Papa François have never been so bad. They put up a wretched fight everywhere. I have taken 25,000 prisoners, 30 colours and a great many guns. I will send you all this. My health is very good. I hope you will have enjoyed yourself at Cherbourg. I have had no letters from you for the last two days. Adio, mio bene. Tout à toi.

NAP.

DRESDEN 29 *Aug.*

It was at Cherbourg, on August 31st, that Marie-Louise was informed of the tragic battle in which her husband and her father were at grips. How did she react to this news?

"A bad cold is weighing heavily upon me", she writes to Méneval, his secretary. "The good news I have received to-day will do much more to restore me than any possible physic. I hope this great victory will bring the Emperor back very soon, and peace with him." And the next day but one, she observes: "Of all the particulars of the fine victory the Emperor has just won, what pleased me most was to hear he ran no danger." What a delusion!

In the first place, following upon the battle of Dresden, he has suffered in his health. Taken with vomiting, he was brought back to the city in a state of absolute prostration. "You are drenched to the skin", an old Grenadier—a *tape-dur*—had observed to him, "you must go back and change."

Reverses now take the place of victories and follow upon each other apace. Oudinot, who was marching on Berlin, was stopped dead, on the

191

23rd, at Gross-Beeren, by Bernadotte and compelled to fall back. General Girard, who had left Magdeburg to reinforce him, had great difficulty in returning to that fortress. On the 26th, Macdonald had a disastrous encounter with Blücher, on the Katzbach. On the 30th, Vandamme's Army Corps, hemmed in at Kulm by Barclay de Tolly, Kleist and Schwarzenberg, lost more than half its force: Cortineau, his second-in-command, managed to escape with the Cavalry.

To these set-backs Napoleon unobtrusively refers when he observes: "My affairs are in pretty good shape." The usual "well" has disappeared.

Ma bonne amie

    I have received all your letters from Cherbourg.[1] My health is very good. I am constantly attending manœuvres. My affairs are in pretty good shape. Have a Te Deum sung, my squadrons dressed over all, and guns fired for the victory at Dresden. Adio, mio bene.

NAP.

BAUZEN 6 *Sept.*

Ma bonne amie

    I am back in Dresden on my return from Sélésie (Silesia), where I drove back the enemy forces. The weather was shocking yesterday. My health is very good. I hope you will have reached Saint-Cloud in good health. Two kisses for the little King. Tout à toi.

NAP.

DRESDEN 8 *Sept.*

---

[1] This word is written over the word *Cayeu.*

The Allied forces are still at the gates of Dresden. On September 2nd, Napoleon delivers an attack against the Russians, who have occupied Gross-Sedlitz and Dohna; he drives them off and halts at nightfall in Dohna. Thence he makes for Liebstadt, via Sedlitz. On the 9th, he spends the night in the old castle of Liebstadt.

Mon amie

I have received your letter from Rouen. I hope your next will tell me you are at Saint-Cloud in good health. Did my son recognize you? Give him a kiss for me. Adieu, mon amie. Tout à toi. NAP.

DOHNA 9 *Sept.*

Mon amie

I have received your letter telling me you have reached Saint-Cloud in good health. I have heard, however, that you had caught a cold. Did your son recognize you and did you find him grown? My health is very good, the weather is fine, autumn is setting in. Adio, mio bene. Tout à toi. NAP.

LIBSTAT[1] 10 *Sept.*

Strange, indeed, is the next letter. Can it be that "Papa François" is stricken with remorse? What other explanation can be given to the fact that a letter to the latter's daughter is sent to Dresden, when the Emperor knows full well she is in France?

Ma bonne amie

I have received your letter. I am glad to see you have recovered your health. I enclose a letter from your father. I opened it by mistake, thinking it

[1] The Sotheby Catalogue has "Liebenstein".

was for me. I did not read it; tell me if there is anything in it that is likely to interest me. You may write to him and to your sisters through the same channel; send your letters to me, I will forward them to him. I am in good health. Adieu, ma douce amie, be content and cheerful. Tout à toi.   NAP.

A kiss to your son, they all tell me he is charming and that you spoil him.

DRESDEN 13 *Sept.*

Mon amie

I have had no letters from you for three days because irregulars have flung themselves on the rear of the army and cut off our communications. I trust this will soon come to an end. My health is very good. My affairs are in good shape. Adio, mio bene.

PETERSVALD 17 *Sept.*   NAP.

Mon amie

You will not have heard from me these last few days because enemy irregulars and deserters have posted themselves in the rear of the army. They will shortly be driven off. My health is good and my affairs are in good shape. Do not be anxious, and keep well. Adieu, ma bonne Louise. Give a kiss to the little King for me. Tout à toi.   NAP.

PETERSVALD 18 *Sept.*

Ma bonne amie

I have received all your letters down to that of September 17th, our communications having been opened up and the irregulars driven off. My health is very good. My affairs are in good shape. Adio, mio bene. A kiss to the little King.   NAP.

HARTA 24 *Sept.*

"The turncoats!" Yes, indeed, now that the glamour of victory has received a blow, now that there is no longer any glory in claiming to belong to the "Grand Army", defections are multiplying. Desertion plays havoc among the Saxon soldiers, at the instigation of Bernadotte, under whom they fought at Wagram, and who secretly sends them proclamations in which he, a Frenchman, urges them to desert the cause of France. A Saxon battalion deserts to him bodily on September 27th. The Westphalians are shaken. The Poles alone are impregnably devoted to Napoleon. But it is important to fill up the voids.

"Madame et chère Amie"—began a letter from the Emperor, dated September 27th—"you will preside over the Senate, and you will deliver the following speech." And a paper drafted in code fell from the letter. It instructed her to have the orators of the Council of State submit and the conservative Senate pass a *senatus-consultum* prescribing a levy of 280,000 conscripts, 160,000 of them as an advance on the 1815 contingent.

"Every Frenchman realizes", declared the Minister Regnault de Saint-Jean d'Angely, "that in the present situation of Europe, the nation can only hope to defend its territory by proportioning its effort to conquer to the efforts put forth to enslave it."

In the Imperial missives, the words "my affairs are in good shape" occur again and again, which shows that they were going badly, all the more so in view of the fact that the illness of the

Major-General of the Army, Berthier, Prince de Neuchâtel, was not calculated to comfort the Emperor.

Mon amie

You may appoint the household as you please. You had better not appoint Courtomer, if it does not suit you. My health is very good. My affairs are in fairly good shape. Give a kiss to my son and never doubt your faithful husband   NAP.

DRESDEN 29 *Sept.*

Ma bonne amie

I enclose 2 letters from Vienna. I duly received your letter of September 28th; all your letters have reached me. I have lost none of them. The month of September was a very rainy one, October, therefore, seems unlikely, in my opinion, to be very fine. The Prince de Neufchâtel is very weak. He is recovering, however, but it will take him a few days longer. My health is very good. Give a kiss to my son. You speak of him in such glowing terms that I long to see him. Adio, mio bene. Tout à toi. NAP.

DRESDEN 5 *Oct.* 2 *a.m.*

Between the 5th and the 26th of October, there is a gap in the Emperor's correspondence. Silence prevails. What a number of events—of painful events—succeeded one another in the meantime! On the 8th, the Bavarian Corps went over to the enemy: General de Wrede had come to terms with the Austrians. In order to hem in Napoleon finally, three armies had converged towards Leipzig, coming up from Silesia, from

" TON - - - - NAP "

The Emperor Napoleon I in his familiar surroundings.

" MA DOUCE AMIE "
Marie-Louise.

Bohemia and from the North, under Blücher, Schwarzenberg and Bernadotte respectively; they were 325,000 strong, while Napoleon has but 214,000 men.

Action was joined from all sides on October 11th. In the North, Marmont has Blücher to contend with; in the West, Bertrand beats Gyulay. But it is more particularly in the South, at Wachau, that the storm rages. Napoleon is holding his own against the Prussians and the Russians, against Kleist, Wittgenstein and Prince Eugène of Wurtemberg. A headlong charge by Murat, Kellerman and Latour-Maubourg is about to break through the enemy's centre, when the Czar sends the Russian Guard, the Prussian Guard and the Cossacks into action. Napoleon holds his own at every point. An informal armistice observed on the following day favours the Allies, who receive reinforcements.

Napoleon has moved nearer to Leipzig. On October 18th, the Probstheida plateau is the key position. Here Lauriston and Victor successfully resist the furious assaults of Schwarzenberg, Kleist and Wittgenstein, who vainly charge again and again. Macdonald, however, has been pushed back by Benningsen. Bernadotte has crossed the Partha with his Swedes, and suddenly, in the midst of the battle, the Saxon and Wurtemberg Corps, 35,000 strong, who served as a link between Napoleon and Ney, go over to the enemy, join Bernadotte and turn their guns against their erstwhile brothers-in-arms. Napoleon moves up with the Household Cavalry to

Ney's assistance. But retreat is imperative.
Napoleon has lost the Battle of the Nations. A
fool of a corporal adds to the disaster by blowing
up the bridge over the Elster before some twenty
thousand men under Macdonald, Poniatowski,
Reynier and Lauriston have had time to cross
over to the other bank. They swell the number
of the prisoners.

How poignant is the short note dated October
25th, in which the Emperor announces his
impending return to Mayence and refers the
Empress to the Bulletins for knowledge of "the
state of his affairs"!

Ma bonne amie
      I shall be in Mayence in a few days' time.
The Bulletins will tell you all about my affairs. My
health is very good. Please give a kiss to the little King
and never doubt the feelings of your faithful husband
    GOTHA 25 *Oct.*   NAP.

Ma bonne Louise
      I have received your letter. I am sorry to
hear you were concerned about the interruption of our
communications. My health is very good. I am
moving back to the Rhine, on my way to Mayence;
my army needs to be refitted and to go into good
winter quarters. Adio, mio bene.
                              NAP.
    VACHA 27 *Oct.*

With Bertrand in the lead and Oudinot bringing up the rear, the French Army falls back,
vigorously pursued by Blücher, while Gyulay on

the left and Yorck on the right cling to its flanks like a pack of wolves. The Bavarian General de Wrede, formerly so proud of the approval of the foremost of the world's soldiers, is in position at Hanau, near Frankfort, on October 30th, when Napoleon appears. Macdonald's sharpshooters, pending the arrival of his guns, come into action. Then, as soon as Drouot's batteries are lined up, the Old Guard move to the attack. Sabred by the Cuirassiers and the Dragoons, Schwarzenberg's Uhlans and the Austrian regiment under Jordis are wiped out. De Wrede is wounded. The rout of the Austro-Bavarians is complete. It is a dangerous thing to attack a wounded lion.

Ma bonne Louise

I have arrived at Frankfort, on my way to Mayence. I gave the Bavarians and Austrians a good thrashing yesterday, the 30th, at Hanau. They were 60,000 strong. I took 6,000 prisoners, some colours and some guns. They were foolish enough to think they would cut me off. My health is very good and has never been better. Adio, mio bene. A kiss to the King. The couriers of the 23rd, 24th and 25th are lost, those of the 26th and 27th are at Mayence. I am expecting them in an hour's time.

NAP.

FRANKFORT 31 *Oct.*

"Madame et très chère épouse", adds an official despatch, "I am sending you twenty stands of colours captured by our armies at the battles of

Wachau, Leipzig and Hanau. It is a tribute it gives me pleasure to pay you."

By November 2nd, Napoleon was in Mayence; the year 1813 alone had witnessed the retreat of the French Army from the banks of the Niemen to the banks of the Rhine. As the result of successive desertions and treasons, the "Grand Army of the Nations" was now reduced to the French Army alone, to the reorganization of which Napoleon, no sooner back in Mayence, applied himself. He knew their worth: "My troops have a decided superiority over the enemy."

Ma bonne Louise

  I wrote to you this morning by the telegraph, to tell you of my arrival at Mayence, in perfect health. I am glad to hear yours is better. All you tell me about your son gives me pleasure; I long to see him, it seems he is quite reasonable. Give him a kiss for me. Adio, mio bene. Tout à toi.

NAP.

MAYENCE 2 *Nov.*

Ma bonne Louise

  I have received your letter of October 30th. The state of your health and the little King's gives me great pleasure. It seems to me they are too much alarmed in Paris. My troops have a decided superiority over the enemy; he will be beaten sooner than he thinks. Be calm and cheerful and laugh at the alarmists. Tout à toi.

NAP.

MAYENCE 3 *Nov.*

Ma bonne amie Louise

I have received your letter of November 1st. You will have heard from me since, and the telegraphic message of the 3rd informs me that you had received the news of the battle of the 30th. My health is very good. I love you and long to see you. I have summoned the Corps législatif to meet on December 2nd. Wait before you give an answer to King Louis until I know what he wants and what he says. Adio, mio dolce amor. Tout à toi.

NAP.

MAYENCE 4 *Nov.*

Mon amie

I have received your letter of November 3rd. I am rejoiced to hear that the fine weather is affecting your health favourably. Mine is perfect. Give a kiss to the little King for me and believe me your faithful husband

NAP.

MAYENCE 5 *Nov.*

Mon amie

I have received your letter of November 3rd. If Louis comes as a French Prince to take his stand next the Throne, I will receive him and forget all the libels he has published about me. If he comes as King of Holland, it is not very nice of him to oblige me to take stern measures just when I have so much to do, but the man is a fool. Pity me for having an ill-mannered family, I who have loaded them up with benefits. My health is very good. I am reorganising my army. Everything is taking shape. Give a kiss to my son. Tout à toi.

MAYENCE 6 *Nov.*

Ma bonne amie

I have received your letter of the 4th. I was glad to see you were happy and in perfect health. Give a kiss to the little King. My health is very good. The weather here is rather cold. The army is being reorganized and re-formed. Adieu, mio ben.

NAP.

MAYENCE 7 *Nov.*

Ma bonne Louise

The Minister of War will hand over to you 20 flags[1] taken at the battles of Leipzig, Vacha and Hanau. You may answer as follows.[2] Ton

NAP.

[*undated*].

The time had come for all Frenchmen to close their ranks and for the members of the Imperial Family to forget their mutual grudges.

The moral of the campaign in Germany was drawn by Napoleon in his reply, on November 10th, in Paris, to a delegation from the Senate.

"All Europe was with us a year ago; now all Europe is against us. This is because world opinion is moulded by France or by England. We should therefore have everything to fear, were it not for the energy and power of the nation. Posterity will bear witness that when mighty and critical circumstances arose, both France and I myself were equal to them."

[1] The words "20 drapeaux" are written over "4 lettres j'ai".
[2] The answer is wanting.

XI

THE CAMPAIGN IN FRANCE
(1814)

THE INVASION

IRRESISTIBLY, the tidal-wave of the invasion was breaking on the frontiers of France. The armies launched in hot pursuit of Napoleon were forging ceaselessly ahead. A composite host of Austrians, Wurtembergers, Russians and Bavarians, the main army under Schwarzenberg and Boubena, in conjunction with the Bohemian army, with its Emperors and Kings, was pouring into Alsace and Franche-Comté by way of Switzerland; Blücher's Saxons, Prussians and Russians—the Silesian army—were sweeping into Lorraine, while an army of Russians, Swedes and Prussians under Bernadotte, Wintzingerod and Bülow, was invading France through Belgium. Without halting to lay siege to places on their way, all these forces made a concerted drive on Paris. Yet another army was coming up from the South; it was composed of English, Portuguese, Spanish and German troops, with Wellington in command, and Marshal Soult was endeavouring to stem its onset, making the most of such natural defences as the rivers in the South of France. In Italy the Allies were held by the line of the Adige, defended by Eugène de Beauharnais.

Napoleon had left garrisons behind in Germany at many of the fortified towns, Dresden, Magdeburg, Danzig, Torgau and Erfurt—islets of vain resistance soon to be submerged; but Napoleon hoped to make good these losses, and that "the call of honour would prove a call to arms", summoning every Frenchman to defend the sacred soil of France. The Senate, however, and the legislature were all for peace—peace, they averred, was "ardently desired by France, essential to humanity".

"Is this a moment to remonstrate with me—when two hundred thousand Cossacks are breaking through our frontiers? What is the 'throne'? A piece of wood, draped with a strip of velvet; surely, to speak the language of a king, *I* am the throne."

And he was determined to defend the throne. Special recruiting officers were despatched post-haste to raise new troops, to constitute a national guard which would act as a reserve. No time could be lost! Epinal had surrendered to fifty Cossacks, Mâcon to fifty Hussars, Rheims to a half-company, Nancy to Blücher's scouts. Langres and Dijon had capitulated. The mere cry "The Cossacks are coming" sufficed to send a wave of terror through the countryside; Paris was panic-stricken.

"To the courage of the National Guard I entrust the Empress and the King of Rome, my wife and child", the Emperor said, addressing the

officers of the National Guard of Paris. Leaving
Marie-Louise as Regent, and his brother, King
Joseph, as her adviser, Napoleon quitted the
capital at 3 a.m. on January 25th, 1814, to resume
command of the Army—a sadly depleted army of
some fifty thousand men, dispersed in and about
Châlons and Vitry-le-François, under Marshals
Ney, Victor, Marmont and Mortier.

The Emperor's plan was to prevent the concentration of the various enemy forces operating
between the Marne and the sources of the Seine.
Starting from Saint-Dizier, he marched on
Brienne—the very town where he had received his
youthful education. He slept at Maizières, in the
house of one of his former teachers, a local curé,
the Père Henriot, who undertook to act as guide.
On January 29th, at Brienne, he launched an
attack on Blücher's Prussians and Alsufief's Russians. The attack, which cost the life of Rear-
Admiral Baste, was successful. The Prussians,
retreating on Bar-sur-Aube, joined forces with
Schwarzenberg's Austrians in the plain. On
February 1st, the Allies joined battle; they outnumbered the French by three to one. The centre
of the French Army, with the Young Guard, was
at La Rothière. Losses on both sides were equal,
but Napoleon ordered a retreat on Troyes. This
explains the advice given to Marie-Louise.

Mon amie

   You ask me whether you should go to the
Opera to hear *l'Oriflamme*. You have gauged my
opinion correctly, you must not do so. So long as the

territory of the Empire is overrun by enemies, you should go to no performance; the only one that would be worthy of you would be to go to St. Genevieve's to pray. You ask me whether you should see the King of Naples and the Queen a second time; no, because I have not seen them again. I shall be at Troyes to-morrow. My health is very good, though the weather to-day is most unpleasant.

Adieu, mon amie. Tout à toi.

NAP.

PINEY 2 *Feb*.

How justifiable was the refusal to receive the King of Naples! And what effrontery was Murat's, when he ventured to approach the Empress after his compact with the enemy! On January 6th, and again on the 11th, did he not sign a pact of alliance with the Courts of London and Vienna—in order to safeguard his throne? He promised to furnish the Allies with 30,000 men, and this force was destined to contribute, in the following month, to the set-back of Prince Eugène de Beauharnais in Italy. On leaving the Viceroy he announced that the time had come to choose between two flags: the flag of Virtue and that of Crime!

"Murat", Napoleon was to say in after-days, at St. Helena, "is a man *I made*, my sister's husband; he owes everything to me, would have come to nothing without me, and his fame is due to me alone: to think it was Murat—of all men—who wrote those words!"

The French Army was dying of hunger. "The Empress is dying of consumption", Napoleon wrote to King Joseph, and advised him "to keep her spirits up"; hence the encouraging tone of these letters:

Mon amie

  I have received your letter, it is very cold to-day. My health is good. Kiss the little King for me. Ton

NAP.

Mon amie

  I have just received your letter of February 4th. I am sorry to hear you are worrying; cheer up and be gay. My health is perfect, my affairs, while none too easy, are not in bad shape; they have improved this last week, and I hope, with the help of God, to bring them to a successful issue.

  Adio, mio bene. Tout à toi.

NAP.

A kiss to the little King.

The 6th, 4 a.m.

But the news of the La Rothière engagement, as published in the *Moniteur* at Paris, had caused widespread anxiety. The Empress had not put in an appearance at the Opera for the first night of *L'Oriflamme.* She issued an order for solemn intercession to be made at the church of Saint-Geneviève, the patron saint of Paris, by whose good offices another invasion was stayed. The Director of Museums applied for sanction to remove the pictures from the Louvre. The bullion at the Treasury was loaded on to wagons which were kept in readiness to start in the Tuileries courtyard. This atmosphere of panic impressed Napoleon.

Mon amie

I have arrived at Nogent and beaten the enemy who was marching on Paris from Chalon and Vitry. I have succeeded in pushing back the main enemy force 3 marches.

My health is good, I am full of hope.

NOGENT *the* 7*th*, 12 *p.m.*

"I had meant to launch an attack on Bar-sur-Aube, against Emperor Alexander", he wrote to King Joseph on February 6th, "but I am sacrificing everything else to the necessity for covering Paris."

He realized that, in the capital, people had "lost their heads".

Mon amie

I have just received the courier of the 6th. Your letter grieves me deeply; it tells me you are discouraged; those who are with you have lost their heads. I am quite well and I hope my affairs will take a turn for the better, but I do beg you to cheer up and take care of yourself; if I were to hear you do not know how to keep well it would distress and hurt me. You know how I love you. Adieu, ma bonne Louise, have courage for those about you.

A kiss to the little King. Tout à toi.

NAP.

The 7*th*, 7 *p.m.*

"I fervently hope", he wrote to his brother, King Joseph, on the same day, "that the departure of the Empress from Paris will not take place. We must not shut our eyes to the fact that the consternation and despair of the populace might have disastrous and tragic results." The exchange of letters continued, and we have Napoleon's answer to his brother despatched that evening. "Paris is not in such straits as the alarmists believe. The evil genius of Talleyrand and those who sought to drug the nation into apathy, have hindered me from summoning it to arms—and see to what pass they have brought us!"

NOGENT-SUR-SEINE, *the 7th, 5 p.m.*

Ma bonne Louise

I realize you must be anxious. But I do beg you not to worry too much. I hope to beat the enemy soon. Several fine Divisions have just reached me. My health is very good and I hope that in a few days' time all will be cleared up. Give a kiss to the little King for me. See the Archbishop and Cambacérès about the ceremony at St. Genevieve's. It must come from you; my opinion is that you should not fail to go there, as a matter of faith; it would have been necessary, however, to have had the clergy, and it would become known. Moreover, I am not sufficiently familiar with such matters; you must ask Méneval about it. Tout à toi.

NAP.

The "uncle" to be consulted is Cardinal Fesch, who solemnized the marriage of the Imperial couple. But her brother-in-law, too, thought fit to proffer advice. "I think, Sire", King Joseph wrote at midnight (on February 8th), "that a service of public intercession at Saint-Geneviève's will fail of good results. The despondency of the public is too deep-seated. As to the Catholics, I beg Your Majesty to take my word for it that so long as the reconciliation with the Vicar of Christ is not publicly recognized, the Government cannot expect anything of them."

There is a faint gleam of hope in a letter written by the Emperor to Marie-Louise on the same day. And the following letter, too, strikes an optimistic note.

Mon amie

I wrote to you three times yesterday, for I am sorry to know you are anxious; I will tell you, as between ourselves, that peace will probably be signed within 4 days; besides the enemy is pushed back from Paris in every direction. They are far too frightened in Paris. Tout à toi.

NAP.

3 *a.m.*

Mon amie

I have received your letter of the 8th. I am glad to hear you are easier in your mind. I do beg you to be cheerful and not to worry, it would harm you and my happiness depends upon knowing you are in good health. Give a kiss to the little King for me. [Adieu].

NAPOL[EON]

NOGENT 9*th*, 3 *a.m.*

Napoleon is counting on the results of a conference between the belligerent Powers, which is taking place at Châtillon-sur-Seine. Caulaincourt attended it as plenipotentiary, with Rumigny as his attaché.

Mon amie

     I have received your letter of February 1st. You were quite right not to go to the Opera; it is not seemly. I reached Troye, you see,[1] in good health, though the weather is rather cold at times. The Congress met to-day, February 9th, at Chatillon-sur-Seine. The Austrians were represented by Stadion, the English by their Foreign Minister and 3 or 4 other negotiators, the Russians by Rasum[ovs]ki. Adieu, mon amie. Tout à toi.

NAP.

TROYES *5 Feb*. 1814

"Lord Aberdeen's attitude seems straightforward and almost conciliatory. But Stadion and Humboldt take a stand of arrogant hostility, while Razumovsky is brutal and implacable." There was no longer any question of the "natural frontiers" of France, as mooted by the Allies at Frankfort; the 1791 frontier was taken as a basis of negotiations. So the conditions of peace had been laid down; an envoy was awaiting the reply.

"We must have peace—and peace at once", Marshal Berthier declared when Napoleon tendered him the fateful document with a despairing gesture. "What! You ask me to sign such a treaty as this, to violate the trust reposed in me

---

[1] The word *ainsi* is written over *ce mardi*.

and—after all our struggles and our victories, after all the blood that has been shed—to leave France smaller than I found her! Impossible! If we abandon the Rhine frontier, it means that France is curtailed!"

That night he never closed his eyes. Constant, his faithful servant, shared his vigil. "Everyone wants peace", Constant observed. "They'll find soon enough", the Emperor answered gruffly, "that it's a dishonourable peace."

After his chief of staff, after his old and trusted servant, his own brother Joseph with "perfect frankness" tendered his advice—in a missive of cold malignity. "You must have the courage to bow to necessity, which leaves you only two alternatives to choose from: death and despair. If you desire peace, make it at any price. If you cannot do so, it is left to you to die with fortitude, like the last emperor of Constantinople." On that day, February 9th, the conference adjourned for ten days. The hopes of peace evaporated while sickness played havoc with Napoleon's little Army, and the Young Guard melted away.

Mon amie

     I agree with you that there is no need for you to go to St. Genevieve's; it would have been a good thing a year ago. My health is very good; do take care of yourself and be brave. The weather is still bad, and the enemy has many sick in consequence. Adieu, ma bonne Louise. Believe in all my love. A kiss to your son.

NAP.

    9 *Feb*.

XII

THE LION'S AWAKENING

On being informed that Blücher is marching on Paris along the Valley of the Marne, Napoleon shakes off in the morning of February 9th the torpor in which defeatist talk has kept him enthralled. He hastens to his maps, bends over them, marks them with pins headed with wax of different colours. To Maret, who brings him the conditions laid down by the Allies, he observes: "That is not the question. I am just working out a way of beating Blücher. He is advancing along the road from Montmiral. I shall beat him to-morrow." And posting Marshal Victor at Nogent-sur-Seine, and Oudinot at Bray, he makes for Sézanne with Ney and Mortier, who are presently joined by Marmont.

On February 10th, in the morning, Marmont crosses the Petit-Morin and delivers a surprise attack on the Russian Corps under Alsufief. Following up the Marshal are conscripts with no other uniform than a coat and a fatigue cap—the so-called "Marie-Louise". Brought to bay along the road from Châlons to Paris, which he has been ordered to cover, Alsufief is crushed. He himself is taken prisoner, together with another general whom Napoleon treats as his guest, that same evening, at an inn in Champaubert, which has given its name to the battle. A sand-pit in which hundreds of dead bodies were piled up was given the name of *la Fosse aux Russes*. A cannon-ball had remained embedded in the front wall of the inn where he spent the night and from which he wrote to Marie-Louise:

Ma bonne Louise

Great *Victory*: I have destroyed 12 Russian regiments, taken 6,000 prisoners, 40 guns, 200 ammunition wagons, captured the Commander-in-Chief and all his Generals; moreover, I have not lost 200 men. Have a salute fired at the Invalides and the news published at every place of entertainment. I am following up Sacken, who is at La Ferté-sous-Jouarre. I expect to reach Montmirail at midnight hard on his heels.

NAP.

CHAMPAUBERT, *the* 10*th*, 7 *p.m.*

Mon amie

I hope you gave 3,000 livres to the courier who brought you the Russian General's sword. You must be generous when couriers bring you good news; you must give them money. When they are officers, diamonds.

I am leaving for Montmirail; I hope to send you some good news to-day. My health is good. Tout à toi.

Ton ami
NAP.

A kiss to my son.

[*undated*]

From the picture by J. J. Schnirer.

BRIENNE
29th January, 1814.

"PAPA FRANÇOIS"
The Emperor Francis I of Austria, 1768-1835,
Father of Marie-Louise.

The next day, when the Emperor's bulletin was received in Paris, cheers broke out. At the Opera, where *Armide* was being performed, the orchestra and the chorus-singers struck up the air of *La Victoire est à nous*.

Victory indeed smiled on the French the next day and the next but one—every day, in fact. On the Brie plateau in the district of Epernay, Montmirail overlooks the valley of the Petit-Morin. Sacken and Yorck are converging upon that townlet when, on February 11th, Napoleon appears and takes up his position at Marchais. Trusting to the fact that the Allied troops outnumber the French three to one, Sacken attacks the village, which is defended by Ney, while Mortier and Friant counter-attack the Russians at l'Epine-au-Bois and Guyot's Cavalry hurl themselves on his rear. The rout of the Prussians and Russians was complete. A famous painting by Horace Vernet depicts the battle just at the moment when under a lowering sky their line is broken by Mortier and by Lefebvre, the husband of Madame Sans-Gêne:

Mon amie

To-day I attacked the large Russian and Prussian enemy forces one league in front of Montmirail. I beat them, put them to flight, took the whole of their artillery, captured 7,000 prisoners, more than 40 guns; not a man of this routed army escaped. I am not feeling very well. Tout à toi. Give a kiss to my son.

NAP.

11*th*, 8 *p.m.*

[In the handwriting of a secretary].

From the farm of l'Epine-sous-Bois, between Montmirail and Vieux-Maisons. Have a salute of 60 guns fired and the news given out at every place of entertainment. General Sacken was killed.

The room from which he wrote this letter was cluttered up with dead bodies which had to be removed to enable the Emperor to take a little rest. The pursuit in the dark had come to an end. Sacken took advantage of this respite to slip away towards Château-Thierry under cover of the Prussian rearguard.

On February 12th, the Emperor sought and attacked him there though outnumbered three to one. An enveloping movement carried out against a Prussian Army Corps gave him possession of the Nesle plateau, a commanding position. Overthrown and with their ranks broken, the Prussian Generals Horn and Jurgass are driven back into the funnel-shaped Valley of Château-Thierry, where their rout adds to the congestion of the retreat. The Russian General Frendenrich, attempting to stem the tide, is sabred and taken prisoner. Yorck's army throngs the approach to the bridges in a confused mass, whose crossing is covered by the battalions of Prince William of Prussia, until they are cut to pieces by a bayonet charge.

FROM THE SUBURB OF CHÂTEAU-THIERRY
12 *Feb.* 1814

I have been in the saddle all day, ma bonne Louise. I have had the whole of the enemy rear-guard captured, 4 Russian and 3 Prussian battalions strong, and two guns. Everything was taken, even the General in command; he is a Russian Major-General. The enemy lost the whole of his artillery, all his baggage and two-thirds of his army, and was compelled to take to flight and cross the Marne at Château-Thierry, on his way to Soissons. All his field hospitals and his line of communication to Châlon and Vitry were captured.

My health is very good. Communications having been opened up with La Ferté-sous-Jouarre, I shall be hearing from you within a few hours' time. Adieu, mon amie, be cheerful and happy.

NAP.

Have all the news I give you published as an article under the heading of Paris.

Ma bonne amie

I am very glad to hear you feel reassured and are easier in your mind. I have spent the day here, having the bridge restored. The Duc de Trévise has just passed through and is following up the enemy, who is fleeing in disorder towards Reims, making for the Ardennes.

My health is good. NAP.

CHÂTEAU-THIERRY, *the* 13*th*, 5 *p.m.*

Leaving Mortier, Duc de Trévise, at Château-Thierry to harry the remains of the beaten army, Napoleon turns against Blücher, who has compelled Marmont to fall back from Etages to Montmirail and is attempting to cut off Marshal Victor, who is posted at Sézanne, from the small Imperial Army. At daybreak on February 14th, Blücher is driving Marmont's four thousand men before him, when, of a sudden, seven thousand cavalry hurl themselves at him. They belong to the Guard. Napoleon has just arrived, with Ney and Nansouty. Beaten in front and outflanked, Blücher and Kleist take to flight in the direction of Janvilliers, where Grouchy charges their flank and Drouot crushes them with grape-shot from his fifty guns. They are driven back to Champaubert, to the defile of the *bois enchanté* of Etages, where Alsufief's Grenadiers had surrendered a few days previously:

Ma bonne Louise

      I have some good news to give you, I have beaten General Kleist, who had 36 battalions with him; I took 8,000 prisoners and killed 4,000 of his troops; I took 10 flags and 3 guns without having more than 200 or 300 dead and wounded. The cavalry of my Guard covered themselves with glory. Have 30 guns fired and an article inserted in the *Moniteur*.

                                 Tout à toi

                                     Nap.

A kiss to my son.

MONTMIRAIL, *the* 14*th*, 9 *p.m.*

In a graphic epitome the *Bulletin Officiel* summed up the operations as follows: "Thus in four days' time, this Silesian Army, comprising the Russian Corps under Sacken and Langeron, the Prussian Corps under Yorck and Kleist, and close upon 80,000 strong, was beaten, dispersed, annihilated."

The Battle of the Marne fought and won, there remained the task of stemming on the Seine the tide of the main Bohemian army which had swept over the Yonne and the Loing, Montargis, Nemours, Fontainebleau, Moret and Nangis. Two Marshals, Oudinot and Victor, are falling back before it when suddenly they are ordered to make a stand. With his guns coming up posthaste, his infantry in wagons, his cavalry at the trot, the Emperor comes up. From the South there push up towards the Seine Kellerman, Treilhard and some troops withdrawn from Spain. On February 16th, Napoleon is at Guignes. He climbs to the top of the bell tower, displaces a few slates with the scabbard of his sword, and looks down into the plain. His plan is formed:

Mon amie
      I received your letter this morning at 10. I was glad to find you were in good health and pleased with your son. Give him a kiss from me. I hope to send you some good news to-morrow.
  My health is very good.
  Adieu, ma bonne Louise.

              Tout à toi
                 Nap.

GUIGNE, *the* 16*th*, 6 *p.m.*

On the 17th, Napoleon marches on Nangis, the meeting point of three roads converging upon Troyes. Here Wittgenstein has three Russian Divisions, those "Tartar monsters who dishonour their Sovereign". "To-morrow, we shall be in Paris, their General has told them." Their fate is settled in a trice. Turned on the left by Keller-man, on the right by Michaud, crushed by Drouot's guns, their squares are broken up, and two Divisions taken prisoner.

Ma bonne Louise

I had two letters written to you on the battle-field to give you some good news. I have taken 6,000 Russian prisoners, I defeated Witgenstein's Corps, taking 15 of his guns and 50 artillery wagons. Several Generals have been captured; my troops are following up the enemy in the direction of Montereau, Provins and Bray. By to-night, the whole of the big enemy army will have retreated across the Seine in great disorder.

Adieu, ma bonne amie. A kiss to my son. I have given the necessary instructions to enable you to have 30 guns fired.

NAP.

NANGIS, *the* 17*th*, 4 *p.m*.

De Wrede occupies Villeneuve-le-Comte with two Bavarian Divisions. Victor would have got the better of them had l'Héritier's Dragoons charged: nor did Napoleon spare the guilty General a resounding reprimand.

On February 18th, the Austrians under Bianchi are attacked at Montereau by General Château, who is beaten off. But Napoleon hastens up with Pajol. From the heights of Surville, over-looking the confluence of the Seine and the Yonne, he himself lays the guns, heedless of danger: "Never fear, my friends, the cannon-ball that

will kill me is not yet cast." The National
Guards from Brittany storm the suburbs of Melun.
And Pajol's Cavalry charge the Austrians and
Wurtembergers so violently that they have not
time to blow up the bridge of Montereau.

Ma bonne Louise

I am feeling tired. I have had a splendid
day; I defeated Bianchi's corps, 2 Divisions strong,
and the Wurtemburgers, I captured 4,000 of them,
killed 2,000, took 6 guns and large quantities of
wagons; best of all I carried the bridge at Montereau
before they could cut it. I debouched on the enemy,
I captured 2 Austrian colours, one General and
several Colonels.

Adieu, mon amie. Tout à toi.

NAP.

MONTEREAU 17 *Feb*. 6 *p.m.*

And how is public opinion affected in Paris?
Rumigny describes to the Emperor the entrance
of the prisoners into the capital: "Twenty
thousand captives have just filed through amid
triumphal cheers. At sight of the bronze column
and the Imperial statue, they all bared their
heads. A great many of them even bowed down
before it." The vile flatterer! Caulaincourt's
brother-in-law, Saint-Aignan, speaks very differ-
ently: the Police Minister, Savary, no longer
claims to have the situation in hand: desertion is
rife; the excitement of some is only equalled by
the dejection of others. It is essential to treat. . . .
Peace!

XIII

PEACE FADES FROM SIGHT

WHEN the Congress of Châtillon-sur-Seine, momentarily suspended, resumed its sittings, Caulaincourt received instructions dated February 17th: "Providence has blessed my arms. Yesterday, I broke up Prince de Schwarzenberg's Army, which I hope to destroy before it has recrossed our frontiers. Your conduct must be the same. You must do everything for peace. I want peace . . . on the basis of the Frankfort proposals."

Only on the 21st did the Imperial despatch reach Caulaincourt, who, in the meantime, incurs the anger of Napoleon by not standing firmly to his guns: "I consider you as being kept in the dark, knowing nothing of my affairs, and influenced by lies", writes Napoleon, on February 19th. "I am so upset by the infamous scheme you have forwarded to me that I already feel dishonoured, merely for putting myself in a position to have the suggestion made to me that I should agree to the frontiers previous to the Revolution."

The day before, at Nangis, Napoleon had been sent an officer under a flag of truce by Schwarzenberg to beg for an armistice. "The despicable

wretches fall on their knees at the first
set-back", he writes to his brother Joseph.
"Now that Fortune is again on my side, I am
free to make my own terms. The enemy is dis-
heartened. I therefore hope to be able to make
peace." It is in this frame of mind that he writes
to Marie-Louise:

Ma bonne amie

My affairs are going so well that Schwart-
zenberg asked me for an armistice last night. I hope
we shall have peace in a few days' time, a lasting
peace, worthy of me and worthy of France. Give a
kiss to my son and believe in all my love.

Adieu, ma bonne Louise. NAP.

NANGIS, *the* 18*th*, 7 *a.m.*

While the Emperor has guns fired in honour of
the victory of Montereau, peace remains his
chief objective and that word occurs in the
glorious bulletin.

Ma bonne amie

I was so tired, last night, that I slept 8 hours
on end. Have 30 guns fired in honour of the fight at
Montreau. It is necessary, when I write to you to
have guns fired, that you should write a letter to the
Minister of War, signed by you, and that you should
tell him of any advantage I write to you about, until
peace is signed, for the Minister of War should always
be informed direct of military developments.

Adieu, ma bonne Louise. NAP.

The 19*th*, *noon*

"The King of Rome praying to God": the portrait was by Mlle. Thibault, who painted a replica to serve for the engraving ordered by Napoleon. "Dress him in the uniform of the National Guard", suggested King Joseph, mixing up in a matter that did not concern him.

Ma bonne amie

You have sent me a very beautiful sweet-meat-box, with the portrait of the King of Rome at prayers. I want you to have it engraved with the caption: "*I beg God to save my father and France.*" This little engraving is so interesting that it will please everybody. I am sending you Mortemart with 10 flags captured from the Russians, the Prussians and the Austrians. My health is good. The Emperors of Russia and Austria, and the King of Prussia were at Pont at Madame's; they had come there from Braye, and their headquarters were to have been at Fontainebleau on the 18th. They are now making post-haste for Troye. My troops have entered Nogent and Sens. Give a kiss to my son, keep well and never doubt all my love.　　　　Nap.

MONTRAU, *the* 20*th*, 9 *a.m.*

Mon amie　　NOGENT-SUR-SEINE 20 *Feb.* 6 *p.m.*

I have arrived here. The weather is terribly cold to-day, which inflicts suffering upon us and has been very useful to the enemy, because all the crossings are very good in that sort of weather, so that he has been able to evacuate everything in the direction of Troyes, without trouble, and without our being able to take half of all he has. My health is good. The Emperor of Austria has not got beyond Troye, the Emperor of Russia was at Bray and wanted to sleep at Fontainebleau.　　*[unsigned]*

Mon amie

I have just received your letter of the 20th at 10 o'clock at night. The portrait of the little King, with the caption *God save my father and France*, should be engraved in 36 hours' time. A well finished copy can be made in 2 minutes. Give orders for it to be on sale in Paris within 48 hours. Adieu, mon amie, tell me your cold has left you and that you are well again.

NAP.

NOGENT 21 [*Feb.* 1814], 4 *p.m.*

The Emperor had put Marshal Augereau, Duc de Castiglione, who had borne himself bravely in Germany, in command of the Army Corps at Lyons. Augereau was to fall on the rear of the enemy forces and capture their convoys, either in the Departments along the frontier—Mont-Blanc (Savoy) and Ain—or along the upper reaches of the Saône. In view of the slackness of his operations, Napoleon instructs Marie-Louise, for the purpose of inspiring him with greater energy, to act upon the young Duchess of Castiglione, Adélaïde-Josephine de Bourlon de Chavanges, whom the Marshal worshipped. Augereau was war-weary. Did he not issue, a few weeks later, the following proclamation, unfortunate for his reputation: "Soldiers, you are released from your oaths by the abdication of a man who, after sacrificing millions of victims to his ruthless ambition, has not consigned himself to a soldier's death."

Mon amie

Have the Duchesse de Castiglione sent for and tell her to write to her husband that he should bestir himself, that he ought already to have freed Mont-Blanc and the Ain Department, and dislodged the enemy; let her write to him to that effect, and urge him to fight well. My health is good, the weather is very fine, but that is about all. Adieu, mon amour. Tout à toi. A kiss to the little King.

NAP.

NOGENT 22 [*Feb.* 1814], 9 *a.m.*

Nevertheless, the hour seemed favourable to peace proposals. Aghast at the sudden swerve of fortune in Napoleon's favour, the Czar discovered that his hair was turning grey. "I have also received proposals from the enemy", King Joseph wrote in answer to a letter. "They read more like a capitulation than terms of peace."

"My Brother, I have entered Troyes", Napoleon wrote on February 24th. "The enemy are deluging me with proposals for an armistice. We may be arranging one this morning; but it cannot be concluded except in so far as the Châtillon negotiations are followed up on the Frankfort lines. The Minister of the Interior (Comte de Montalivet) is a milksop; neither he nor the Police Minister (Savary) knows France any better than I know China!"

Such was the Emperor's mood when he wrote to Marie-Louise to try to encourage "Papa François" to develop a will of his own, instead of being a mere tool of the Allies.

Ma bonne amie

The weather is very cold. I am slightly fatigued. I am drawing near the Marne, falling back to Pont-sur-Seine. "Papa François" was at Troye, very sad and worried and seeing but little of the Russians. They are not very fond of each other. The French like the Austrians better than the rest of them. My health is good. I give you a kiss. Adieu, mon amour.

PONT 24 [*Feb*. 1814], 8 *p.m.*   NAP.

Ma bonne Louise

The cold weather here is most painful for poor soldiers, who are obliged to be in the saddle night and day. Your father was at Troyes, very downcast and rather ill, he did not see much of the Russians—they do not like him. You had better write to him complaining that he does not let you hear from him, that he has forgotten you, and that, while serving the interests of his monarchy, he might help us, that he should be reasonable and have a will of his own and not be the instrument of England and Russia. In short, write him a strong letter commending to him your interests and those of your son. Tell him at the same time that we are determined to die rather than agree to a shameful and unfair peace, which, moreover, would be bad policy, for it would not last. Adieu, mon amie. Tout à toi.   NAP.

TROYES 25 [*Feb*. 1814], 2 *p.m.*

My troops have entered Bar-sur-Seine and Vandeuvres. I am very pleased with my people. They are filled with enthusiasm and keenness. They kill a great many of their enemies peacemeal. The Cossacks commit horrors. The Emperor Alexander is much hated here. Your father is esteemed and better liked, but he always declared he could do nothing. He spent the day walking about in his garden, went out rarely and saw but few people.

Ma bonne Louise

The weather is still very cold, to-day, though I was hoping it would become milder. My health is very good. I hope to hear from you that the little King is well and that he has got rid of his cold. My troops are at *Bar-sur-Aube* and at *Châtillon-sur-Seine*. It appears your father does not like the Russians; he sees the Emperor Alexander but very rarely. They are negotiating a truce; I do not know whether they will be successful. Adieu, ma bonne Louise. Tout à toi.

NAP.

Keep well, a kiss to the little King.

TROYE 26 [*Feb.* 1814], 3 *p.m.*

TROYE 26, 6 *p.m.*

Ma bonne amie

I am master of Châtillon-sur-Seine. So that the Congress the Allies intended to hold in my country is now under my control. It was through vain-glory that they determined to hold the Congress in Burgundy. My troops are at Bar-sur-Aube, at Châtillon, at Auxerre. Marshal Auger[eau] is march-ing on Dijon. No armistice has yet been signed. We are not agreed as to the line of demarcation. It would be impossible for the disposition of the inhabi-tants and peasantry to be better. They come forward to a man.

The Russians tried to put forward the Bourbons. They were laughed at everywhere, and no one would second them. On this point the Austrians did not second them, nor would they hear of the Bourbons.

Adieu, mon amie. I give you a loving kiss.

NAP.

Mon amie

I have received no letter from you to-day, nor any newspapers either. I am moving to the vicinity of Brie-Contre-Aubert[1]. My health is very good. I hope to be soon rid of all our enemies, [or] at least [to have driven them] many marches from Paris. Tout à toi. Ton fidèle

NAP.

Give a kiss to my son.

Ma bonne amie

I have received your letter of the 28th. I have sent you your father's letter. A worthy and upright man, he is so often led astray. All this will turn to his confusion, but meanwhile he is injuring us a great deal [il nous en fait beaucoup].

It has been raining all day to-day. I have captured some baggage, taken 3 or 400 prisoners and driven back the enemy to the right bank of the Marne. We will see what can be done to-morrow. Adieu, ma bonne Louise, keep well and give a kiss to my son.

JOUARRE I *March*, 6 *p.m.* NAP.

Confidence in the future is the keynote of the Emperor's letters. An armistice may be concluded at any moment. Peasants and townsfolk alike, roused to action by the invasion and its menace, are flocking to the standards. Napoleon hopes very soon to be "rid of all our enemies", and expresses his sympathy for the "fine, honest man", his father-in-law, who has been so frequently betrayed.

[1] The name is written over Cha . . .

Let us see how on that very day (March 1st) his honest father-in-law responded to the Emperor's sympathy. Suspected by his allies of half-heartedness, he had to sign a solemn declaration binding him for twenty years. Each of the four Allies, England, Austria, Prussia and Russia, undertook to keep up an army of 150,000 men for the duration of hostilities. This prelude to the Holy Alliance—for the league of four laid claim to "holiness"—was the work of Lord Castlereagh.

The Emperor's letters show that he had no cognizance of this event. Indeed, next day, on March 2nd, we find him urging his wife to write to the Emperor of Austria, and ask him to be "a little on our side".

Marie-Louise responded to the Emperor's love, but in the manner of a spoilt, capricious child. "I got up in a very bad temper to-day", she had written in her travel diary a little time before. "I have no news from the Emperor. He is so casual in his ways. I can see he is forgetting me. Oh, it's only women who are really constant in their love; men are so unreliable."

While the future of France—her own, as well—is trembling in the balance, how does *La Régente* pass her time? She amuses herself with the prattle of a parrot given her by the Duchesse de Montebello; with sketching, embroidery and music. She sends her dear Duchesse, la Maréchale de Montebello, "a masterpiece begun a year ago, a lovely kerchief!" And she sends her "bouquets" as well as wagers lost at gambling. But meanwhile, like the medieval *châtelaines*, she and her maids of honour are busy shredding linen for the wounded. For is it not a woman's proper task to play the ministering angel to suffering men?

But what a host of other things preoccupy her! Questions of etiquette; the entrées to the Court which must be granted to the Duchesse Savary de Rovigo, *née* Marie-Charlotte-Félicité de Faudoas-Barbazan de Seguenville; the scenes made by the governess of the Enfant de France, Madame de Montesquiou; all the tittle-tattle, false or true, that is going on about this or that "red", "black", or "white" lady of the Court. It is with such trivialities that Marie-Louise regales her husband at the very moment when his throne is tottering to its fall. Napoleon, answering her letters amid the din and turmoil of the battlefield, takes the opportunity of inculcating some admirable lessons of philosophy, not to say morality.

Ma bonne amie

     I have just received your letter of March 1st. I was sorry to hear that Madame Montesquiou had made a scene that annoyed you; it was a piece of forgetfulness on her part; she is so good to the little King that you will forget it and always be kind to her. What has been said about Mme Anatole is very ill-natured; such talk is infamous, for nothing more is needed to bring into ridicule and contempt worthy and deserving people who are highly virtuous and quite blameless. The Duchess, who is such an upright woman, should be the first to disapprove of such ill-natured talk, which affects women's happiness so deeply. It would be better to stab such young women with a knife than to countenance such rumours, which dishonour them and make them ridiculous and repulsive.

It rained a great deal yesterday. I consider it unnecessary for you to give the entrée to Madame la Duchesse de Rovigo. Write to your father and urge him to be a little bit on our side, and not to listen merely to the Russians. The enemy is falling back on La Ferté-Milon. My health is good. Adieu, mon amie.

NAP.

JOUARRE 2 *March, noon*

Mon amie

Send for the Duc de Cadore. Tell him to have a list drawn up of all the pallets, straw-mattresses, sheets, mattresses and blankets I have at Fontainebleau, Compiègne, Rambouillet, and in my several mansions, and that are not needed in my Household—there must be at least a thousand—and to give them over to the military hospitals. My affairs are going well. I am expecting favourable results promptly. Adieu, ma bonne Louise.

NAP.

LA FERTÉ-SOUS-JOUARRE 2 *March, 6 p.m.*

FERTÉ-SOUS-JOUARRE 3 [*March*], 8 *a.m.*

Ma bonne Louise

I have received your letter of the 2nd. I am sorry to see you pay attention to silly people. Never argue with anybody; it is unworthy of you. It was ill-mannered of Madame Montesquiou to lose her temper in your presence. If she had a quarrel with the Duchess, they should have had it out away from you; never argue with Madame Momorancy. It all smacks of small-minded women, and is unworthy of your nature. Never argue with any one about all

From the picture by Delaroche.

DEFEAT

Fontainebleau, April 1814.

THE KING OF ROME

Napoleon Francis Joseph Charles, son of Napoleon I
and Marie Louise (afterwards for a few days Napoleon II,
and later known as Duke of Reichstadt.)

this, but hold the Minister of Police and all the Ministers at a distance. In this country people are only too ready to eat out of your hand. Above all be cheerful and look after your health. Mine is good. Adieu, mon amie. Tout à toi.

NAP.

How is it that Marie-Louise failed to realize the unseemliness of writing to Caroline Bonaparte, Queen of Naples, after the perfidy of Murat, her husband? For Napoleon had learnt, twelve days before, on unimpeachable authority, that his brother-in-law, in order to retain the throne of Naples, had gone over to the enemy.

Mon amie

You ask me whether you should write to the Queen of Naples. My answer is *No*: she behaved improperly towards me, who of a mere nobody made a Queen. My health is good. I am pursuing Bluker, who is much exposed. Be contented and cheerful, my affairs are going pretty well. Tout à toi.

NAP.

BÉRUT-SAINT-GERMAIN 4 *March*

After his defeat Blücher had fallen back through Reims on Châlons, where Langeron's two divisions, coming from Mayence, had joined him. At the same time a third great army, the Northern Army, after crossing Belgium, had entered the battle area; it was composed of Russian troops led by Wintzingerod, Voronzov and Strogonov, and Bülow's Prussian Division.

Napoleon marched against these new adversaries. At 4 a.m. on March 5th, Generals Corbineau and Laferrière launched a surprise attack
on the four enemy battalions garrisoning Reims,
and took them prisoner.

Mon amie

      I am off to Béry-le-bas, on the way from
Laon to Rheims. I have relieved Rheims, taking
4,000 prisoners and 600 baggage waggons. Have a
salvo of 30 guns fired. I will write to you this evening.
Adieu, ma bonne Louise. Tout à toi.   NAP.

  FISMES, *5th*, 10 *a.m.*

Nansouty stormed the bridge at Berry-au-Bac
and two hundred troopers led by Colonel Prince
Gargarin were added to the tale of prisoners.

Ma bonne Louise

      I crossed the bridge over the Aine here
this afternoon. I routed those who attempted to
oppose me, capturing 200 horse and Prince Gargarin,
who was in command. I also took 2 guns. My
vanguard is half-way to Laen (Laon). My health is
very good. Bulcher (Blücher) was wounded, they
tell me. Tout à toi.   NAP.

  BERY-AU-BAC, *5th*, 7 *p.m.*

On March 6th, the capture of the Craonne
heights, by the Young Guard, preceded the
general engagement with the Russians on the
following day. The only way of access to the
Craonne plateau was through a defile a hundred
fathoms wide. The plateau itself was protected

by three ravines, and the Russians were covering the defile with sixty guns. Nevertheless Victor, at the head of the Young Guard, stormed the position. Drouot forced his way through with the artillery, while Ney debouched on the enemy's right wing. Nansouty then brought up his cavalry. The result was a Russian defeat; but not an overwhelming one.

Ma bonne Louise

Yesterday I attacked and thoroughly defeated the Russian Army under Vinzigerode, Voronsow and Langeron, 30,000 strong. I pursued them for 5 hours, from Crean to l'Ange-Gardien. I killed 3 or 400 of their troops, capturing 2,000 and several guns. I had 600 killed or wounded. The Duc de Bellune and General Grouchi were wounded. I am marching on Laon. I am in good health, though somewhat fatigued. The weather is very cold. Adieu, mon amie. Tout à toi.

NAP.

BRAY-SUR-AISNE, *the 8th*, 7 *a.m.*

I wrote to you this morning from Braie, ma bonne Louise, but I hope this letter will reach you first, for it is going by way of Soissons, from which I have driven out the enemy. Yesterday, I defeated the Russian Army under Winzigerod, Langeron and Voronzof. I wrote to you to have 30 guns fired in consequence. My health is good, though the weather is very cold this morning. I am marching on Laon. Adieu, ma bonne amie; a kiss to the little King. Tout à toi.

NAP.

L'ANGE-GARDIEN, *the 8th*, 11 *a.m.*

The "Auberge de l'Ange Gardien", where the Emperor's letter was written, was situated at some cross-roads on the highway from Soissons

to Laon. It was here that Generals Sacken and
Langeron endeavoured to intercept Marmont's
Army Corps, which had been vanquished by
Yorck at Athies. From the summit of the Laon
heights Blücher had watched the battle. It was
impossible for Napoleon to force the enemy's
positions.

Ma bonne amie

I am forwarding to you a letter from your
father. I opened it by mistake, tell me what is in it
if it is likely to interest me. I am in good health,
though rather fatigued. The enemy is posted in very
strong positions at Laon, where he is hiding. Give a
kiss to my son, and never doubt all my sentiments.

CHAVIGNON, *the* 10*th*, 8 *a.m.*   NAPOLEON

Marie-Louise made no secret of her displeasure
at the opening of her mail ostensibly "by
mistake". "I send you a bouquet and an opened
letter", she wrote to the Duchesse de Montebello.
"Don't conclude that I am getting into the
Emperor's charming ways; I opened it only on
the orders of the person who wrote it, because it
contained a letter for me as well."

The letters she received from the Emperor
were so hard to decipher that she called in King
Joseph to help her, "as we have got to have the
news the Emperor sends published in the newspapers". As a result an intimacy grew up
between them, to which Napoleon took exception; Joseph "has the reputation of loose ways
with women. Keep him at a distance". "King

Joseph says very tiresome things to me", Marie-
Louise wrote to the Duchesse de Montebello.
What exactly did she mean by "tiresome"? And
was there good reason for Napoleon's tone of
deep distress?

Mon amie

      I have received your letter. Do not be too
familiar with the King; keep him at a distance, never
allow him to enter your private apartments, receive
him ceremoniously as Cambacérès does, and when in
the drawing-room do not let him play the part of
adviser as to your behaviour and mode of life, you
manage better than he does. I approve of your going
to the terrass by the underground passage. What
the King says is nonsense and in any case it is not the
business of the public. I hope you are not altering
your manner of life in any way; it is perfect, mar-
vellous, and has earned you the esteem of everybody;
you have, therefore, only to go on as you have been
doing. When the King attempts to give you advice,
which it is not his business to do, as I am not far away
from you, you should break off the subject and talk
of something else and be cold to him. Be very
reserved in your manner to the King; no intimacy,
and whenever you can do so, talk to him in presence
of the Duchess and by a window. This, however, is
not absolutely necessary. But do not allow him to
interfere too much in what is no concern of his and in
your household affairs, which never are. Adieu, mon
amie. The weather is very bad. Tout à toi. Nap.

    soissons 11 *March*, 3 *p.m.*

Ma bonne Louise

      I have received your last letter. I am for-
warding your letter to your father, through the outposts. I am sorry you showed the King your father's

letter and his (your ?) reply. You trust him too much.
Such communications should be made to no one but
me. Every one has betrayed me. Will it be my fate
to be betrayed by the King? I should not be surprised
if such was to be the case, nor would it break down my
fortitude; the only thing that could shake it would be
if you had any intercourse with him behind my back
and if you were no longer to me what you have been.
Mistrust the King; he has an evil reputation with
women and an ambition which has become habitual
with him in Spain; and if you wish to please me and
not make me unhappy, show the King none of my
letters, or of your father's, or of your own answers.
Keep him at a distance. They tell me the King has
conceived the insensate and guilty intention of having
addresses sent me in favour of peace. Were this to
be done, I should be very angry; it would lead to
nothing and it would spoil all France's affairs. Why
do you speak to me of this? I say it again, keep the
King away from your trust and from yourself, if you
care for my satisfaction and happiness. All this
depresses me rather; I need to be comforted by the
members of my family, but as a rule I get nothing but
vexation from that quarter. On your part, however,
it would be both unexpected and unbearable. Adieu,
mon amie. Tout à toi. NAP.

SOISSONS, *the* 12*th*, 3 *p.m.*

On the same day Napoleon wrote as follows to
Méneval, who had apprized him of King Joseph's
intrigues: "I have received your letter; your reply
was a good one. I shall treat as an act of rebellion
the first address soliciting peace that is presented
me." Thus Joseph, who had sought to probe his
brother's intentions through the medium of his
secretary, was duly warned. He had tried to

induce Marie-Louise herself to take a similar step. The following letter, in which Napoleon definitely states that he will not be dictated to by anyone, relates to the same topic.

Ma bonne Louise

I have received your letter of March 12th, which gave me pleasure because I saw that you have no secrets from me and that you do not allow yourself to be led. You were quite right to refuse to send somebody. I would have received him very badly. I do not need to have any one professing to concern himself more than I do with the interests of the people. I know better than anybody what suits France, and if at all possible I will make peace. My health is very good. Adieu, ma bonne amie. A kiss to my son. Tout à toi.

NAP.

SOISSONS, 13 *March*, 3 *a.m.*

Mon amie

I thank you for the beautiful and precious watch-chain you have sent to me. I have received your two letters. The King is intriguing; he will be the first to suffer; he is a pygmy, swelling with his own importance. Without honour and a sense of duty a man can accomplish nothing. I recognized your beautiful soul in your letter and in the love you bear me. I cannot conceive how I can have distressed you, it distresses me very much, but I wanted to write to you plainly, so as to avoid all unpleasantness. Adieu, ma bonne Louise. You know how I value your judgment and your character, and above all how deeply I love you. Tout à toi, ton fidèle

NAP.

RHEIMS, *the* 14*th, noon*

I have defeated the Russian and Prussian Corps under St. Priest, capturing 25 guns, 5,000 men; the Commander-in-Chief St. Priest was mortally wounded. Have salute of 30 guns fired.

Ma bonne Louise

I have received your letter of the 13th. I was very sorry to hear you were grieved. I am sorry not to have spared you that bad time, for you are so perfect and so good that one is always in the wrong. I have a very bad cold to-day. The weather is shocking—cold and damp—and it has a bad effect. I am hoping, however, that we shall at last have warmer weather. Pray be cheerful and contented, and keep in good health, you know how necessary that is to my happiness. Adieu, mon ami. Give a kiss to the little King. Tout à toi. NAP.

RHEIMS, *the* 14*th*, 2 *p.m.*

Ma bonne Louise

I have received your letter of yesterday. I was glad to see your health was better. I am grieved to think you should have had any sorrow I might have spared you. My health is good. I am still here, which is a good thing for my Old Guard. It gives them a little rest. My troops will enter Châlons and Epernay this evening. Adieu, ma douce amie. A kiss to the little King. Tout à toi. NAP.

RHEIMS, *the* 15*th*, 3 *p.m.*

The Emperor is grieved to learn that Marie-Louise has been distressed by his admonitions. It was his duty to warn her against King Joseph's intrigues—"a pygmy swelling with his own importance. Without honour and a sense of duty a man can accomplish nothing." A reflection worthy of Corneille, and obviously inspired by the classics.

And here is another sentiment of the same order, in a despatch sent to King Joseph on March 16th. "Whatever happens, you must not allow the Empress and the King of Rome to fall into the enemy's hands. . . . Stay with my son and do not forget that I would sooner see him drowned in the Seine than captured by the enemies of France. The tale of Astyanax, captive of the Greeks, has always struck me as the saddest page of history."

Such, however, was to be the tragic destiny of Napoleon II, the *Aiglon*. "I shall find him quite grown up," the Emperor writes. He was never to see him again!

Ma bonne Louise

    I received your letter of March 15th at 10 o'clock at night. I am glad to see your health is better. Mine is good. My troops have entered Châlons; these days of rest are doing me good. Give a little kiss to my son. All you tell me about him leads me to hope that I shall find him much grown; he will soon be turned three. Tout à toi.   Nap.

RHEIMS, *the 16th, 3 p.m.*

Ma bonne Louise

    I have received your letter. I hope the weather in Paris is as fine as it is at Rheims. It will be very convenient for your outings and will do good to your health. Give a kiss to the King and never doubt the love I bear you. Ton   Nap.

I am going to Epernai this afternoon.

RHEIMS, *the 17th, midday*

Mon amie

I received no letter from you yesterday. The weather has at last become very fine again.

I am moving forward to have a hit at the enemy. My health is very good. Adieu, mon amie. Tout à toi.

NAP.

A kiss to the little King.

EPERNAI, *the* 18*th*, 8 *p.m.*

A letter for King Joseph left at the same time as this mild letter to the Empress.

"My brother, I reached Epernay this evening and to-morrow, before daybreak, I shall set out for Arcis-sur-Aube, where I shall be on the 19th, at noon. I shall throw three bridges over the river and, according to circumstances, advance either on Méry or on Troyes, so as to take the enemy in the rear. This means that the Duc de Tarente (Macdonald) will have to dispute every inch of ground. The Duc de Raguse (Marmont) has stayed at Béry-le-Bac; the Duc de Trévise (Mortier) is at Rheims, and General Charpentier at Soissons. I am leaving Brigadier-General Vincent at Epernay; he is in charge of all the mass-levies. I do not think it likely that Blücher, who has had a good drubbing, will be able to make a move before two days. He will then have to cross the Aisne, and the Duc de Raguse, as well as the Duc de Trévise, will put up a stubborn resistance against him. My advance will throw the enemy's rearguard into the utmost confusion."

What rashness thus to unmask his plans!

Mon amie

I forcibly crossed the Aube and the Seine yesterday. I gained possession of Méry; I cut the road from Paris to Troye; I took a fine pontoon equipment from the enemy, who has evacuated Nogent, Vitry, and the entire bank of the Aube. My affairs [are going] well. My health is good, the weather is fine. Write and tell your father that the idea of compelling us to make peace by humiliating us and taking Antwerp from us is impracticable, that the nation has energy, especially the peasants, that they will eventually be beaten, with the Empire more powerful than ever, that you entreat him not to sacrifice the Empire to England's greed, and to take into consideration not the passions of Stadion and the rest of them, but the interests of his monarchy, the welfare of his family, the peace and quietness of his life; let him make peace on the basis of Frankfort; it will be secure, and is the only one conformable with the interests of his monarchy; tell him to beware lest he be compelled, in a few months' time, to make peace on unf[avourable] terms; to be quite sure that nothing will lead the Emperor to give up anything, for at Châtillon they would again declare it insufficient.[1] Tout à toi.

NAP.

PLANCY, 20 *March*, I *a.m.*

After receiving her husband's letter, the Empress sent him the following rather colourless reply, dated March 21st, 10 p.m. It was intercepted by the Allies' scouts.

"*Mon cher Ami*

" I got your letter of March 20th, from Plancy, this evening. I am very pleased to hear that you are satisfied with the turn events are

---

[1] "rien ne portera l'Empereur à se désister d'avoir quelque chose que l'on dira impossible à Châtillon."

taking. I do hope that everything will go on now as you would wish. Anyhow, that is my most fervent wish. Mon cher Ami, I would like you to be as happy as you deserve to be. Paris is buzzing with good news. It seems that much has been added to the news brought in by your messengers—so much so that there is talk of many victories, and, above all, of prospects of peace. I have written to my father as you desired, but, as it is rather late, I fear I shall not have time to make a copy of the letter. You shall have it to-morrow; I will send it to you by the eleven o'clock courier. I would like to think that my letters will bring good results—but I doubt it. My father hardly pays any attention to me, in dealing with affairs of State. The Archchancellor (Cambacérès) struck me to-day as very heroic. He spoke to me of his courage in a most amazing way. I have not been able to see King Joseph; he hardly ever comes to see me in the morning nowadays. And I am very glad of it, as I think you would rather it were so.

"Your son sends you a kiss; he is in splendid health. He slept very badly last night; he had a terribly restless night, and cried a great deal in his sleep. We asked him what had been the matter. He said that he had dreamed of his dear papa, but wouldn't say what he dreamed. We could not get him to tell us anything whatever about it. I am in excellent health; this spring weather suits me perfectly. For two years I have noticed that the winter cold did not agree with me. The days have been so mild that I have been able to go out riding. It has done me a great deal of good; but what would do me most good of all would be to see you again and to know that all my anxieties are over.

"I love you, and kiss you tenderly.

"Ta fidèle amie,

"LOUISE."

The letter sent to "Papa François" runs: "Your army may well be beaten, for the Emperor's army is finer and stronger than ever. You may find yourselves obliged to conclude peace on much less easy terms. Thus you are sacrificing the interests of your monarchy and your prospects of a happy life."

On March 24th, at Doulevant, Caulaincourt made a final effort to persuade Napoleon to write to his father-in-law. He went so far as to submit a draft letter. "My aspirations are too pacific not to approximate to those of Your Majesty and, as I would wish to think, to those of Your Majesty's allies. . . . I am quite ready to despatch my Minister for Foreign Affairs and I can assure Your Majesty that the peace we all so ardently desire would be the work of a few days . . ."

"Such offers are quite futile", Napoleon replied. "You wish to humiliate me to no purpose; Metternich wants peace as little as Alexander does. Alexander's ambition is to march through my capital at the head of his Guards."

"The pen must supplement the sword", Caulaincourt muttered.

"Only the sword", Napoleon retorted, "can decide the present conflict—one way or the other."

But the pen was destined to betray the sword, as we shall see.

XIV

THE EMPEROR BETRAYED BY ONE OF HIS LETTERS

NAPOLEON's skilful manœuvring kept the final issue in doubt until suddenly a mischance brought matters to a head. Napoleon was betrayed by his loving sentiments. On March 24th, Marie-Louise wrote to the Duchesse de Montebello: "I have just heard that the courier of the 23rd was captured. What a misadventure! It angers me!" And well it might! The courier was the bearer of extremely important news:

Mon amie

  I have been in the saddle all the last few days. On the 20th I took Arcis-sur-Aube. The enemy attacked me there at 6 o'clock in the evening; I beat him the same day, killing 400[0]. I took 2 of his guns; he took 2 of mine, which leaves us quits. On the 21st, the enemy army formed up in battle array for the purpose of covering the advance of his convoys towards Brienne and Bar-sur-Aube. I decided to make for the Marne and his line of communications, in order to push him back further from Paris and draw nearer to his fortress. I shall be at Saint-Dizier this afternoon. Adieu, mon amie. A kiss to my son.

NAP.

[*undated*]

Apologizing with ironical politeness for having opened the letter, the Prussian General—Blücher —forwarded it to its destination, "laying it at the feet of the august daughter of His Majesty the Emperor of Austria". The Allies were now fully informed. Napoleon was turning his back to the capital. The road to Paris was free. The tide of invasion promptly swept along it. The Minister of Police, Savary, to whom Marie-Louise related the mishap, failed to discern its frightful consequences; he did not warn the Emperor, but allowed him to be overwhelmed by fatality.

Refer to the Memoirs of the Aide-de-camp, Comte de Ségur. On March 24th, the catastrophe begins. Whereas all the Allied forces are converging on Paris, the Emperor fancies he is keeping them at a distance by taking them in the rear. He pushes his Light Cavalry towards Bar-sur-Aube, his Guard towards Brienne, thus separating the Emperor of Austria—who beats a precipitate retreat towards Dijon—from Schwarzenberg, his Commander-in-Chief.

To the Empress Napoleon sends victorious notes:

Mon amie

I have arrived at Chalons. The weather is cold. Instead of 12 hours, I was 18 hours on the road. My health is very good. I am going to Vitry, 6 leagues from here. Adieu, mon amie. Tout à toi.

Nap.

CHALONS, *the 26th*, 9 *a.m.*

247

Ma chère Louise

I have been 5 or 6 days without news of you. Those wretched Cossacks are the cause of this. I am drawing nearer to you and I hope to hear from you to-morrow. I gave the enemy a good thrashing yesterday. I am anxious to have news of you. Tout à toi.   NAP.

BAR-SUR-AUBE 28 *March*

"The enemy" is the Russian Corps under Wintzingerode—a mere curtain, a make-believe of an army, behind which Napoleon, to his amazement, discovers nothing. What can be happening?

An Army Order issued by the enemy Commander-in-Chief falls into the hands of Macdonald, who brings it to the Emperor. It announces the victory of the Allies at La Fère-Champenoise, the flight of Marshals Marmont and Mortier, and, on their heels, the advance of the Allied forces on Paris. Napoleon refuses to credit the information. "Impossible. In this account everything is false and absurd. See here. The victory they claim refers to March 25th and they have dated it the 29th, whereas it is but the 27th to-day." Macdonald is nonplussed. But Drouot shrewdly opines: "The error in the date is but apparent. It is a misprint, a six put upside down." Without a word, Napoleon takes the paper in his hand once more and examines it carefully. "Quite right", he says, "that changes everything."

The enemy has indeed stolen a march on him:

he is striking at the heart of France. Paris is the vital centre of the country. Consumed with anxiety, the Emperor remains the whole night (March 27th–28th) poring over his maps. His choice falls upon the road from Troyes. Along this, covered by the Seine, he will march to relieve the capital.

Marie-Louise left on the 29th for Rambouillet, and then for Troyes. . . . "In leaving Paris, you lose your crown", groans Queen Hortense. "I will not leave home", shrieks the little King of Rome. "Papa being away, I am the master." "Parisians, I am staying with you", proclaims King Joseph. "Let us arm to protect the city, its monuments, its wealth, our wives and children, all that is dear to us." And the very next day, the *Pygmy* takes to flight.

The Marshals—Mortier and Marmont—agree to a capitulation, which is signed on March 31st, at 5 a.m. Convened by Talleyrand, the Senate decides upon the formation of a Provisional Government. "A flood of abuse, slander and calumny took the place of the marks of respect and devotion formerly carried to the point of adulation. All sense of independence was cast off by the majority of the official bodies." The Allies marched into Paris with green sprigs in their bonnets or shakos, and white armlets. "I will treat no further with Napoleon", declared the Czar, Alexander, when accepting Talleyrand's hospitality.

Informed the same day, at Fontainebleau, of the Empress's departure, and at Essonnes of the battle that has started, the Emperor, who is impatient to reach Paris, catches sight near Athis of a troop of cavalry—Mortier's advance guard. "Halt!" he commands. "How comes it you are here? Where is the enemy? Where is the Army? Who is guarding Paris? Where is the Empress? Joseph? Clarke? How about Montmartre? What about my soldiers?"

"The Army?" replied General Belliard. "It is made up of workmen, Polytechnicians, the National Guard; twenty-eight thousand foot, who held out for some little time against one hundred and twenty thousand men. Montmartre? Devoid of artillery. Joseph? In flight. The troops? They have left the capital."

"They have all lost their heads, then", roars Napoleon. "Very well, we must go to Paris."

"Too late", declares Caulaincourt, dejectedly.

And the Emperor, overwhelmed, sits down, at three o'clock in the morning, at a table in the Cour de France post-house to write:

Mon amie

I came here to defend Paris; but it was too late. The city had been surrendered in the evening. I am assembling my army in the direction of Fontainebleau. My health is good. I suffer at the thought of what you must suffer.

Nap.

THE COURT OF FRANCE 31 *March,* 3 *a.m.*

Then he proceeds to Fontainebleau.

From the portrait by Sir Thomas Lawrence.

METTERNICH

After his elevation as Prince of the Empire.

ABDICATION

Fontainebleau, April 4th, 1814.

Ma bonne Louise

I have had no letter from you. I fear you must be taking the fall of Paris too much to heart. I beg you to be brave and to take care of your health, which is so precious to me. Mine is good. Give a kiss to the little King and love me always. Ton

FONTAINEBLEAU 31 *March*   NAP.

When dealing with the tragic days of the crossing of the Beresina, we saw with what delicacy Napoleon concealed the horror thereof from his wife. In the moral distress of a man who had been all-powerful, his first thought was to inspire her with courage and resignation.

Ma bonne Louise

I was very sorry indeed to hear from your letter that you were ill at ease and worrying. I beg you to compose yourself and to keep in good health; you know how vital it is to my happiness that I should know you are easy in your mind. I will arrange that we meet as soon as possible. My health is very good. Give a kiss to my son and never doubt [ton] NAP.

FONTAINEBLEAU 2 *April*

Ma bonne Louise

I have received your letters of April 1st and 2nd. I hope to-day's rest at Blois will have restored you and dispelled your fatigue. I am very anxious about your health; you take things so much to heart that I fear you may not be able to bear up under it; that is part of my worries. Do try and take heart and keep well. Give a kiss to my son and never doubt my sentiments.   NAP.

FONTAINEBLEAU 3 *April*, 3 *p.m.*

251

But what advice was he to give to her?

Mon amie

The auditor Paravicini has just arrived and given me news of you. You may: (*a*) remain at Blois; (*b*) send me whom you please and take things upon yourself; (*c*) issue proclamations and call meetings, as the provisional Government of Paris does; (*d*) write a very strong letter to your father, commending yourself and your son to his care; send the Duke de Cadore to Vienna. Make it clear to your father that the time has come for him to help us. Adieu, mon amie, keep in good health. Tout à toi.

NAP.

FONT[AINEBLEAU] 3 *April*, 6 *p.m.*

The Emperor is dismayed. To an offer of abdication, the reply of the Czar, Alexander, of which Caulaincourt is the bearer, is as follows: "But what is to be done with the Emperor? The father is an insuperable obstacle to the recognition of the son."

While Caulaincourt is wrapped in silent consternation, the military chiefs, assembled in an adjoining room, lose their tempers and declare that an end must be made of the matter; further submission would be carrying obedience to the point of servility; the Emperor has no right to involve everybody in his downfall; having moulded his destiny himself, it is for him alone to bear the evil consequences.

And Marshal Ney, spurred on by this vehemence, makes for the Emperor's private study: "Sire", he declares bluntly, "it is time to make an end of it! Your situation is that of a sick man whom there is no hope of saving. You must draw up your will and abdicate in favour of the King of Rome."

The thrust goes home. The father must sacrifice himself for his son. It is for the grandfather, for the Emperor of Austria to intervene in favour of the grandson. "Long live the Emperor!" shouted the Old Guard, at the idea of marching on Paris. But how about these others—the Excellencies, the Dukes, the Marshals? The Emperor has learned his lesson. On the 4th, he signs the Act of Abdication:

"The Allied Powers having proclaimed that the Emperor Napoleon was the sole obstacle to the restoration of order in Europe, the Emperor Napoleon, faithful to his oath, declares himself prepared to descend from the throne, to leave France, nay, to give up his very life for the country's good, which is bound up with the rights of his son, with those of the Empress's Regency, and the upholding of the laws of the Empire. Drafted in our Palace at Fontainebleau, April 4th, 1814."

And the next day, the Emperor declares his decision in the Army Orders: "A soldier shares the good and the evil fortunes of his General, his honour and his religion. . . . The Emperor's honour will never be in contradiction with the happiness of France." He himself is no longer anything. His last hope lies in the appeal to the Emperor of Austria, which is to be made by Champagny, Duc de Cadore, the bearer of a petition from the Empress: "Once more, my

beloved Father, I beg you to have pity on me. I
entrust to you the welfare of what is dearest to
me—my son. . . . I should be so glad to be able
to say, later on, that it is to you he owes his
happiness, his peace, as well as those of his father
and of her who kisses your hands very lovingly."

Napoleon is anxious to know what the Emperor Francis will reply. Colonel Gallois sets out
with a further letter for Marie-Louise.

Ma bonne Louise

   I have received your letter of April 6th.
I am glad to hear that your health is bearing up. I am
very much concerned about you and my son, you may
well suppose; I am but little about myself. My
health is good. Give a kiss to my son and write to
your father every day, so that he may know where you
are. Adieu, ma bonne Louise, it grieves my heart
to think of your trouble. Tout à toi.   Nap.

 fontainebleau 7 *April*

Next day, April 8th, Napoleon sends to his
faithful Méneval, whom he has appointed as
secretary to Marie-Louise, a letter in code,
instinct with the deepest dejection. Ségur, his
aide-de-camp, was acquainted with its terms: the
Emperor observed that anything was to be
expected, *even his death*. And he ordered the
recipient of the letter to burn it after reading it
and to make use of its contents with due dis-
cretion. The act of one about to die, thinks
Méneval; and he awaits with the utmost anxiety
further news from Fontainebleau. It arrived on
the next day and the next day but one.

Mon amie

I have received your letter of the 7th. I was glad to see your health was better than was to be expected considering the anxiety you must feel. A truce has been agreed upon, and one of the Russian Emperor's Aides-de-camp was to join you for the purpose of escorting you to this place; but I sent word to you to stay at Orleans, as I myself was on the point of setting out pending such time as Colincourt shall have settled affairs with the Allies. It was Russia's wish that I should be given the sovereignty over the Island of Elba and that I should remain there, and that you should have Tuscany for your son after you, which would have enabled you to be with me as long as it suited you and to live in a pleasant country, favourable to your health. But Schwarzenberg objects to this in the name of your father. It appears that your father is our deadliest enemy. So I do not know what has been settled. I am sorry to have nothing left but to have you share in my evil fortunes. I would have put an end to my life if I had not thought that would but double your misfortunes and make them heavier to bear. If Madame Montesquiou wishes to finish the King's education, she is free to do so, but she must not lay too great sacrifices upon herself. I suppose Madame Mesgrigny (?) is returning to Paris. I do not know what the Duchess will wish to do, I fancy, however, that she will first wish to accompany you. You must have 1,000,000 given to King Joseph, and the same amount to King Louis, to [King] Jerome, to Madame, and to the Princesses Pauline and Elisa, which accounts for the 6,000,000. Issue a decree to that effect, and let the Princesses proceed to Marseilles and Nice, via Limours, which upsets your arrangements. Your State Councillors and Ministers may return to Paris. Take 1,000,000 in gold with you in your coach. Have the same amount conveyed in the King's. Submit a scheme to me for reducing your Household to such of them as are willing and necessary to you. Two ladies are sufficient to have with you. It will make travelling easier. Beauharnais and Ald[obrandini] will follow later. Have their wages paid to all, down to July 1st, including those who are to follow you. We shall travel with the Court teams and the saddle-horses.

Adieu, ma bonne Louise. I pity you. Write to your father and ask to be given Tuscany for yourself. As for me I want nothing but the Island of Elba.

Adio, mon amie, give a kiss to your son.

[unsigned]

Mon amie

I have just received your letter of the 8th, delivered by a courier who had set out on the 8th, at 2 o'clock in the afternoon. St.-Aignan and the Emperor of Russia's Aide-de-camp had arrived, so said this courier, an hour before he set out. You will therefore have been to Orleans this morning; you may stop there if you are travelling with your post-horses, and if you wish[1] to come on to this place, you may do so, but I am writing to you this evening by the courier you sent me. How I sympathize with all your troubles, and fear lest it should impair your health. A kiss to your son. Tout à toi.   NAP.

FONTAINEBLEAU, *the 9th, 5 p.m.*

The closing words—"if you wish to come"— so poignant because they leave to the Empress a decision which the Emperor at bay desires with all his heart, give us an inkling of the motive for the letter in code which has upset Méneval so deeply. Will Marie-Louise seize upon the opportunity afforded her? "My duty is to stand beside

---

[1] Written over "and it is necessary for you".

the Emperor", she declares, "at a time when he must be so unhappy. I will join him and I shall be happy anywhere, provided I am with him." Her tire-woman, Madame de Luçay, a model of married love, who on two occasions had risked her life, during the Terror, to save her husband, has secretly prevailed upon her to leave for Fontainebleau. One day, Marie-Louise emerges in all haste from her dressing-room, crosses a terrace and throws herself into the arms of Madame de Montesquiou, a rigid person, unbending in the observance of all the virtues, which she holds in high esteem. She is about to leave.

A coach awaits her at the foot of a secret stair-case, when a person is announced, whose nefarious influence has but too great a hold on the weak Marie-Louise. The Empress, perturbed by this unexpected development, hid her tire-woman, Madame de Luçay, in an adjoining closet, where she was able to hear every word of the conversation that ensued. And the treacherous adviser succeeded in transforming into a cowardly deser-tion the high-minded resolution of Marie-Louise to bestow upon her husband the comfort of her presence. General de Ségur, who was told of this incident by Madame de Luçay, his mother-in-law, does not put a name to this evil counsellor.

With Marie-Louise the Emperor has a man worthy of all trust, who owes him his fortune. "When shall you get married, Méneval?" he had asked one day. And when his secretary con-fessed his reluctance to marry a woman who would bring him everything: "Is she young, pretty, lovable?" "Yes, Sire." "What is her fortune, tell me, for you to hesitate?" "Two hundred thousand francs, Sire." "I will give you the same amount. And now see you marry her."

It is thus easy to realize with what an easy mind Napoleon, on April 10th, asks Méneval for a piece of confidential information. "Try to penetrate the real intentions of the Empress, and to find out whether she prefers to follow the Emperor amid all the hazards of his ill fortune, or to retire, either to a State which would be given to her, or to the Court of her father, together with her son."

Napoleon is reduced to applying to a secretary as to the decision his wife will come to! And meanwhile Metternich is doing his best to disunite them, to separate them from each other. Bausset, whom he has entrusted with a letter to be delivered to the Empress at Orleans, passes through Fontainebleau, where he receives another from the Emperor:

Ma bonne amie

I have received your letter. Your troubles are all graven in my heart; they are the only ones I cannot bear. Do try and live down adversity. This evening, I will send you the arrangement that has been made. I am given the Island of Elba; you and your son, Parma, Piacenza and Guastella. This means 400,000 souls and an income of 3 or 4 millions. You are to have at least one mansion and a beautiful country (to live in) when you tire of my Island of Elba and I begin to bore you, as I can but do when I am older and you still young. Meternich is in Paris. I do not know where your father is. You should contrive to see him on your way. If you cannot have Tuscany and your fate is settled, ask him to give you the Principality of Lucca, Massa, Carra[ra] and the Enclaves, and furthermore for your Principality to have an outlet on the sea. I am sending Foulet to see about all the terms. As soon as all is done with, I shall go to Briard, where you will join me and we will proceed, via Moulin, [and] Chamberi, to Parma, and then embark at La Spezzia. Aldobrandini will accompany you during the journey. I approve of all the arrangements you are making for the little King; if Mme Boubers will come, she would be suitable for bringing him up. My health is good, my courage unimpaired, especially if you will be content with my ill-fortune and if you think you can still be happy in sharing it. Adieu, mon amie. I think of you, and your troubles weigh heavily upon me. Tout à toi.

FONTAINEBLEAU, *the* 11*th*, 9 *a.m.* NAP.

In the afternoon, on April 11th, Napoleon receives a letter from Marie-Louise, which "wrings his very soul", so precarious does the Empress's health appear to him.

Mon amie

I have just received your letter of the 11th, this morning. Your anxiety and the state of your health wrings my soul. Tell me whether the plan of going together to Parma suits you; you would proceed thence to the spas at Lucca or at Pisa. Enquire of Corvisart which of these spas is more likely to agree with you. Beausset will deliver this letter; you will receive another which I will write to you when I have seen Caulaincourt whom I am expecting to-night. My health is very good. I am full of courage; why is yours not like it? I would willingly share mine with

you. Your letters are replete with the sentiments
that fill your heart; they touch me profoundly and
comfort me; I wish I could do as much for you. I am
having Menevalle written to. Adieu, ma bonne
Louise, my misfortune vexes me more for your sake
than for mine. Tout à toi.

[*unsigned*]

FONTAINEBLEAU, *the* 11*th*, 7 *p.m.*

At the same time—7 p.m.—the Emperor sends
his instructions to Méneval, to whom he has
already written in the morning, as regards the
arrangements to be made for the departure of
the Empress. Husband and wife would journey
together to Parma, as slowly as the Empress's
health might require. "Ask Corvisart what Spa
would agree with the Empress best. Lucca?
Pisa?" Only two "red" ladies (ladies in purple)
were to be taken and the "white" ladies (ladies in
white dresses) who are to remain in the Empress's
service. "Madame de Montesquiou also must
only take with her such attendants as are required
for the King of Rome."

"Must." . . . But is Napoleon still master of
the destinies of his family? Metternich's letter,
delivered to her by Baron de Bausset, brings her
the assurance that she and her son are to be given
an independent existence. Let her repair to
Austria, at least momentarily: such a step would
be in accordance with her August Father's intentions. For the Empress, the painful alternative is
whether to join her father or her husband. A
letter from Napoleon renders this alternative more
tragic.

Mon amie

I have received your letter in reply [to the one] Fouler delivered to you. I am very much concerned at hearing you are so dejected and in such bad health. I hope my ministrations and the expression of sentiments I bear you will do you good and restore your health. I am expecting Caulaincourt. I will write to you immediately. They offer to give me back a battalion of my Guard, 100 strong [in][1] Provence and thence in the Island of Elba. We will travel as slowly as your health requires. Adieu, ma bonne Louise, the change in my fortunes only affects me on your account. Love me well and never doubt

ton   NAP.

I fancy we might meet at Briard or Gien, whence we would proceed by way of Italy or Provence.

FONTAINEBLEAU, *the* 12*th*, 10 *a.m.*

The particulars of the journey in common into exile are thus taking shape. What will be the Empress's decision?

While Baron Méneval, the *secretaire des commandements*, beholds the sufferings of Marie-Louise, the Aide-de-camp, Comte de Ségur, witnesses the Emperor's agony. "Adieu, ma bonne Louise." Is the parting to be for ever?

On April 12th, Caulaincourt, attended by Macdonald and the Czar's aide-de-camp, Shuvalov, brought to the Emperor, at Fontainebleau, the Treaty concluded the day before which was tantamount to his abdication. There remained for him to sign it.

Night was closing in. Napoleon, unattended,

[1] What was written originally was "at St. . . ."

and without saying a word, had shut himself up in his private apartments. Alarmed by his dejected appearance, everyone anxiously awaited developments. The Comte de Turenne had been careful to unload his pistols and put them out of his reach.

Napoleon asked for them. By his irritation, his annoyance at finding them empty, Turenne at once realized that he had been tempted to make use of them. Yet he had been heard to say: "To kill oneself is the death of a gambler. I am condemned to live. Besides, the dead alone never come back!" In his distress, there comes to him a last revulsion of pride: "I have been faithful to my declaration that I would never sign a humiliating peace. I abdicate but yield nothing."

The evening of April 12th comes to an end amid the most frightful dejection. When about to sign his final downfall, the Emperor has fallen into so deep a meditation that, his eyes staring, he already seems to be in another world. When he emerges from it, he calmly discusses the cases of suicide that have marked the end of other great men, his compeers, and to define their reasons, according to the diversity of ages and beliefs. His attendants become more and more anxious.

At eleven o'clock at night, the silence in the Palace at Fontainebleau is suddenly broken by people coming and going. The valet, Hubert, who sleeps in a closet adjoining his master's bedroom, has heard Napoleon pour some drops into a glass of water and gulp it down in all haste. He listens in anguish. Silence, at first, presently followed by groans. The Emperor has attempted to poison himself with a powder he has been keeping in his dressing-case ever since the retreat from Russia. The Duc de Vicence, Caulaincourt, and the Duc de Bassano, Maret, hasten to the spot, followed by the physician Yvan.

"Death will not have me", declares the sufferer to the physician; "you know what I have taken."

With the help of compresses and hot beverages, Yvan fights the effects of the poison, which is finally ejected. But so upset is the physician that he sinks into an arm-chair and has a fit of hysterics; after which, his head bare, he flees on a horse tied to the Palace gates. "It is contrary to the will of God", the Emperor at last declares. And he signs his abdication.

Of this tragic scene nothing transpires, save a deep disgust with mankind, in the letter written the night after.

Ma bonne Louise

     I am sending you General Flaaut [Flahaut], who will give you news of me and bring back news of you. I know your health is not good and I fear travelling at night must have fatigued you. I myself am well and longing for the time to come when we can set out. They tell me the climate is very fine in the Island of Elba. I am so disgusted with men that I am determined no longer to have my happiness depend upon them. You alone can affect it. Adieu, mon amie, a kiss to the little King, kind regards to your father; ask him to be good to us. Tout à toi.

FONTAINEBLEAU, *the* 14*th*, 1 *a.m.*   N ᴀ ᴘ.

"Kind regards to your father; beg him to be good to us!" Now the day before, from Troyes, the Emperor of Austria wrote to Metternich: "What is most important is to send the Emperor away from France, and God grant he may be sent very far!"

How tragic, therefore, must have been the interview between the Emperor Francis and Marie-Louise, the pleading of the wife in favour of her husband, the result of which Napoleon awaited anxiously to hear.

Ma bonne Louise

You must have met your father by this time. They say you are going to Trianon for the purpose, I wish you to come to Fontainebleau tomorrow, so that we may set out together for that land of sanctuary and rest, where I shall be happy, provided you can make up your mind to be so and to forget worldly greatness. Give a kiss to my son and believe in

ton

FONTAINEBLEAU, *the* 15*th*, 4 *p.m.*   NAP.

I have heard here through the courier, and through Flaaut, whom I sent to you yesterday.

Some hearts, however, kept their loyalty intact. Isabey, the Court Painter, had not forgotten the happy days when he painted the portraits of the First Consul, of the Emperor, of Marie-Louise and the King of Rome. He went to Rambouillet to visit the Empress, and thence to Fontainebleau to meet the Emperor. He writes as follows: "As soon as he saw me the Emperor took some steps in my direction; overcome by emotion, I sank on to my knees and clasped his hand. 'Come now', Napoleon said graciously, drawing me to my feet, 'for me everything is over, but, as for you,

264

you owe it to your family to go on with your work.' Then he called to Constant and told him to bring the snuff-box bearing a likeness of Marie-Louise. 'Have this portrait fitted on to a pocket-book so that I can carry it next my heart, and never let it leave my person. Send it back at once, but keep the snuff-box in memory of me.' "

"I want you to come to Fontainebleau to-morrow." But Marie-Louise did not come. Her interview with her father had settled things for her. On that day, April 16th, the Emperor's thoughts strayed back to the deserted wife, whose secret memory still lingered in his heart. "In my exile I will replace the sword by the pen. The history of my reign will be a curious one; I have been seen hitherto only in profile; now I will show myself full figure. What a number of things I have to reveal—things and people regarding whom the world has been misled! I have loaded thousands of worthless creatures with favours—and in these last days what have they done for me? Betrayed me—one and all! Good-bye, ma bonne Joséphine, learn resignation as I have learned it, and never banish from your memory the one who has never forgotten, never will forget you. Adieu, Joséphine."

They were never to meet again.

The letter to Josephine was found some days later in the Emperor's desk at Fontainebleau, and immediately published under the title: "Napoleon's Farewell to Josephine." There was also a farewell to Marie-Louise, which ran as follows:

"*My dear wife,*

"Since Providence, whose purpose I have hitherto misunderstood, has given its verdict against me and in favour of my enemies, and, lacking men, money and munitions, I can no longer fight against it and subdue its will to mine, I am constrained to yield to force. . . .

"I congratulate you on the course you adopted; it was not fitting that you should await your father's visit at the foot of a throne occupied by another. We may be abased by those very persons who have done most to raise us up; but we should never demean ourselves. . . .

"I have no idea what the future holds in store for you, but whatever it be, I hardly think that destiny will bring us together again. And the thought is agony to me. Of all the punishments that Heaven could inflict on me, most cruel is my separation from you. . . . I would make only one reproach to you: Why did you not help me with your advice? Why not exercise the empire on my heart your motherhood conferred on you? You feared me—and you loved me!"

Is this letter authentic? I think so. It is in keeping with the Imperial tradition, which involved the use of *vous* in place of the familiar *tu* in official letters written with an eye to posterity. It explains the Austrian Emperor's visit to Rambouillet as due to his daughter's refusal to come to Paris. But, if the reasons for the father's visit to his daughter are comprehensible, why should the other monarchs have accompanied him?

266

"It is incredible", Napoleon writes to Méneval on April 18th at 5 a.m., "that the Emperor of Austria did not realize the impropriety of bringing the Russian Emperor and the King of Prussia to Rambouillet, above all, when the Empress was ill." Marie-Louise shared his opinion. But the monarchs overrode it, much to the annoyance of Napoleon, who, however, qualifies his general disapproval with a hint of eulogy for the Czar.

Ma bonne Louise

  I have received your letter of the 18th through Laplace; all he tells me has moved me deeply, and the hope that your health will overcome all the vexations of fate bears me up. Isabé has brought me a portrait of you—the one in which you are holding your son in your arms. I think I shall at last be able to set out to-morrow, and I hope to reach the isle of rest before May 1st. Have Méneval send an article on that island written by an Engineer Officer who lived there for 3 years. I am sorry to hear people are indiscreet enough to weary you by untimely visits in view of the condition of your heart. Adieu, mon amie, love me and never doubt the sentiments of

          ton   Nap.

FONTAINEBLEAU 19 *April*, 3 *p.m.*

Ma bonne Louise

  Buisson has just brought me your letter of April 18th. I am sending him back for further news; he will join me at Briare, where I shall put up, to-morrow, for the night, and he will give me full particulars of your meeting with the Emperor Alexander. I pity you for having to receive such a visit, yet as he is devoid neither of tact nor of wit, I hope he will say nothing but pleasant things to you; but I do pity you for having to receive the King of Prussia, who is as likely as not, albeit unintentionally, to say unseemly things to you. I am sorry to see you deviate from the lines of the spas, to which it would be natural for you to go. At all events, I beg you to take care of your health and to be brave, so as to maintain your rank and face misfortune firmly and with courage.

Adieu, ma bonne Louise. Tout à toi. I will send you young Montesquiou to-night.   [*unsigned*]

FONTAINEBLEAU, *the* 19*th*, 4 *o'clock*

Ma bonne Louise

I am sending back Montesquiou, at his mother's request, and I am entrusting him with this letter; he will give you news of me. I am leaving to-morrow at 9 o'clock in the morning, and shall put up for the night at Briard, where I hope to receive a letter from you before morning. I shall travel by way of Nevers, Moulins, Lyons and Avignon. I am sorry to say I shall be a few days without hearing from you. I hope you are in good health, that you will be brave and uphold the honour of your rank and of my destiny, without minding the hard blows Fate has dealt us lately. Give a kiss to my son. Take care of him. Adieu, ma douce amie. Tout à toi pour la vie.

NAP.

FONTAINEBLEAU, *the* 19*th*, 11 *p.m.*

On the same day Napoleon informed Méneval of the route he was to follow on his melancholy progress into exile—the Lyons road through the Bourbonnais, and then the Saint-Tropez road, *via* Avignon and Aix. "The Emperor would like to have news of the Empress to-morrow at Briare, where he is to sleep." And, enclosing an account of the Island of Elba which an engineer officer has just brought to Fontainebleau, he

From the painting by Horace Vernet.

FAREWELL

(Fontainebleau, April 20th, 1814.)

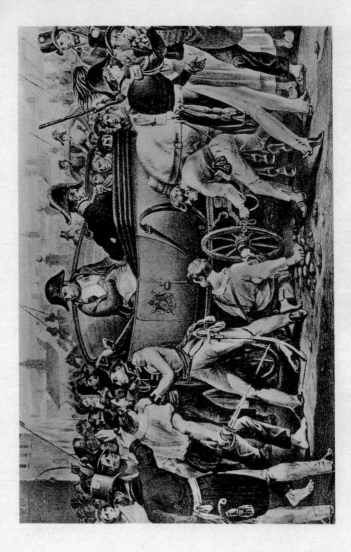

THE WAY TO ELBA

Napoleon's journey into exile, April-May, 1814.

appends a disillusioned afterthought: "You might show it to the Empress, if you think it would interest her."

On April 20th, at eleven, after his touching farewell to the Old Guard—a favourite theme with artists—in the courtyard of the Fontaine-bleau Palace, known since that memorable leave-taking as the *Cour des Adieux*, Napoleon stepped into the *dormeuse de voyage* which was to take him to a humble sanctuary in the "Isle of rest".

Ma bonne Louise

Montesquiou has handed me your letter; the state of your health distresses me very much. Try and bear up and take care of yourself for my sake and that of your son. Go direct to the Spa and try to avoid Vienna in this way. Méneval is being written to about many matters; have him show you the letter and give orders accordingly. My health is good. Laplace has doubtless delivered to you a letter from me; he left at six o'clock in the evening. I will write to you to-night. I do not think I shall be leaving before to-morrow [and then only] if everything is ready. Adieu, chère Louise, love me, think of your best friend and of your son. Kiss him for me.

NAP.

If what they say is true, the conduct of Aldo-brandini and Beauharnais is frightful and dishonours them and their heirs. Tell me about it in a few words. I cannot believe in such infamy.

A melancholy postscript! For, even amongst those most closely associated with Marie-Louise, some had "turned their coats". Bausset, the Préfet du Palais, went over to the Bourbons, and from Baron d'Empire became once more a Marquis. Madame Brignole was now the faithful friend of Talleyrand, Prince de Bénévent, as whose agent she acted in dealing with the Empress. No sooner had Madame de Montebello come to Blois than she emphatically declared she would never go to Elba; her one desire was to return *chez elle*. Saint-Aignan and Doctor Corvisart followed her instructions, which the medical man obligingly embodied in "doctor's orders". Beauharnais, Claude de Beauharnais, *Chevalier d'Honneur*, resigned from the post he held under the Empress; while Prince Eugène de Beauharnais was about to join the King, his father-in-law, in Bavaria, where he became Duc de Leuchtenberg and the first peer of Bavaria.

BRIARD 21 *April, noon*

Ma bonne Louise

Laplace will deliver this letter to you. He is an excellent young man. He will tell you I am in good health. I am going to St.-Tropez; I am leaving in an hour's time, I shall not stop on the way, I fancy I shall be there within 4 days. I am very satisfied with the disposition of the population who show me considerable attachment . . . (?) and love. I have had no letter from you since the 18th. The Palace quarter-master has not arrived, which I put down to the lack of horses. Adieu, mon amie, keep in good health. Give a kiss to my son and never doubt

NAP.

The Emperor is on the road to exile, accompanied by the faithful Bertrand, followed by English, Austrian, Prussian and Russian Commissaries, and attended by an escort of twenty-five troopers. This escort was by no means super-fluous. The man who, in other days, had ridden gloriously beneath triumphal arches was greeted at Avignon with cries of hatred and savage imprecations; so aggressive was the populace that the Commissaries were obliged to intervene. At Orgon and Lambesc there were similar scenes. At Saint-Cannat the Emperor's coach was stoned and its windows were broken. As the party was passing Aix the Sous-préfet had the gates of the town closed, so as to restrain the populace from pouring forth to vent their animosity. On April 28th, the Emperor reached Saint-Raphael, disillusioned, but at last immune from hostile demonstrations. By the irony of fate the ship on which he embarked was the *Undaunted*. On the previous day, at Fréjus, he had written a harrow-ing letter to Marie-Louise, but, on the day he sailed, he was cheered by a letter from his wife, and hope flamed up again.

Ma bonne Louise

I reached Fréjus 2 hours ago. I was well pleased with the disposition of France as far as Avignon; but since Avignon I have found people very much inflamed against me. I was very satisfied with the Commissioners, particularly the Austrian and the Russian Generals; tell your father this. I am leaving for Elba in two hours' time, and will write to you from there. My health is good, my courage undaunted; it could be weakened only by the thought that mon amie no longer loves me. Give a kiss to my son. The Princess Pauline, who is in a Château, two leagues distant, declares she is determined to come to the Island of Elba to keep me company. But she is so ill that I do not know whether she will be able to bear the journey. I have the Grand Marshal and my Aide-de-camp Drouot with me.

Your faithful [husband]

NAP.

FRÉJUS 27 *April*, 3 *p.m.*

Ma bonne amie

I have received your letter of the 23rd, informing me that you were going to Grosbois and to continue your journey from that point. Your father wrote to me from Rambulet [Rambouillet], a fortnight ago; I have just sent him the enclosed reply. I intend, in two hours' time, to go on board an English frigate, which will take me across to the island in a very few days, and from there I will write to you, by way of Livorno, through the Viceroy. My health is good, the weather is fine and I shall have a smooth passage. I hope your health will remain good and that you will have the necessary courage. I shall be very glad to see both you and my son. Deliver the enclosed letter to Corvisart.

Adieu, ma bonne Louise. Pray give a very loving kiss to my son and give my kind regards to all the ladies. Tout à toi.

Your affectionate and faithful husband

NAPOLEON

FRÉJUS 28 *April*

The letter from the Austrian Emperor to which Napoleon refers was written at Rambouillet on April 16th; there is a marked stiffness in the phraseology.

"*Monsieur mon frère et cher beau-fils*, the

affectionate solicitude I feel towards my daughter, the Empress, has prompted me to arrange a meeting with her here. I have been with her a few hours and it is only too clear to me that her health has worsened grievously since I last saw her. I have decided to propose that she should pass some months in the bosom of her family. Her need of rest and quietness is urgent, and Your Majesty has given her too many proofs of real attachment for me to doubt that you will share my wishes on the subject and approve of my decision. Once she has regained her health, my daughter will proceed to assume the sovereignty of her country, and this will naturally bring her nearer to Your Majesty's place of abode. It is superfluous, I take it, for me to assure Your Majesty that her son will be accepted as a member of my family, and that during his residence in my dominions he will enjoy his mother's constant care. *Recevez, Monsieur mon Frère, l'assurance de ma considération très distinguée.*" The letter is signed by the Emperor, but the style is definitely Metternich's; especially the stiff formality of the concluding sentence, the conventional ending of a French business letter.

On Easter Day Vienna was illuminated to celebrate the Allies' entry into Paris. An antiquated gig, inscribed "*Postal Service from Paris to . . .*" had served to convey the news to the Austrian capital. The bringer of the news was Count Fürstenberg, and, with much clacking of whips, a hundred postilions accompanied his progress. "So there we have the outcome of all

Napoleon's victories", wrote the Baronne du Montet. "Paris is in the hands of the foreigner. Under Louis XIV the very worst defeat could not have brought about so dire a catastrophe!" The Baronne, who had accompanied the de la Boute-tières, her parents, into exile, in the days of the *émigrés*, indulges in a veritable pean. "Was ever miracle more impressive, or justice more Draconian? On the very spot where stood the scaffold of our holy King, another altar, composed of battle trophies, has been set up, under the eyes of all the Kings of Europe. When a nation's hour of expiation strikes, it has the sound of a knell for the people it concerns."

Such was the mental atmosphere of the Austrian capital to which Marie-Louise was presently to go.

XV

ELBA AND THE HUNDRED DAYS

THE conquerors of the man who had been master of all Western Europe granted him, out of charity, a crumb of kingship—11,380 subjects in all, according to the *Gazetteer of Elba* published that year. Napoleon's first impressions of the island were agreeable.

Ma bonne Louise

I was 4 days at sea in calm weather. I did not suffer in the least; I have arrived in the Island of Elba, which is very pretty. The accommodation is but middling. I will have a home fitted up in a very few weeks. I have had no letter from you. It is my daily sorrow. My health is very good. Adieu, mon amie; you are far away, but my thoughts are with my Louise. A loving kiss to my son. Tout à toi.

NAP.

PORTOFERAYO 4 *May*

Ma bonne Louise

General Keller, who has come here with me and with whom I was extremely pleased, is going back. I am sending this letter through him; pray write to your father asking him to do something to show his gratitude to this General, who has been most considerate. I have now been here 5 days; I am having fairly nice quarters fitted up, with a garden and in very good air; I shall be there in 3 days' time. My health is perfect; the island is healthy, the inhabitants are apparently of a kindly disposition. What is wanting is to hear from you and to know you are well; I have been without news of you since the letter you wrote to me and which reached me at Ferjus.

Adieu, mon amie; give a kiss to my son and never doubt

ton   NAP.

PORTOFERAJO 9 *May*

Despite the distant attitude his father-in-law had adopted at the turning-point of his career, Napoleon bore him no ill-feeling. And he does justice to the Austrian General who, during the voyage on the English frigate, showed the fallen Emperor the respect that was his due. Perhaps he might enjoy his life once more, if only Marie-Louise would deign to come and share it.

Ma bonne Louise

I have received your letter No. 8 and 11, dated June 22nd, the rest have gone astray. The news you give me of your health and of my son gives me great pleasure. I think you should come as soon as possible to Tuscany, where there are very good waters, much like those of Aix en Savoie. It will have every advantage: you will be nearer Parma, you will be able to have your son with you and you will give nobody any trouble. Your visit to Aix has nothing but disadvantages. If this letter finds you there, remain only for the season, and come on to Tuscany

for your health. My health is good, my feelings
towards you are ever the same and my desire to see
you and prove this to you is very great. Adieu, ma
bonne amie; a loving kiss to my son. Tout à toi.

NAP.

3 *July* 1814

He longed for his wife's presence. He reserved
the best rooms for her use, all of them cool and
charming; six rooms she was to have in the old
Spanish citadel at Porto Longone, overlooking
the sea. He added a storey to his house at Porto-
ferrajo. Everything would be ready in August.
"Write and tell Méneval", he said to Bertrand,
"that I am expecting the Empress here at the end
of August, that I wish her to bring my son, and
that it seems strange I have no news from her . . .
that no one has any rights over the Empress and
her son."

Marie-Louise was writing less often. She sent
a letter, by way of Parma, on July 31st. On
August 10th, masking the ugly fact of her deser-
tion of her husband with loving protestations and
promises to join him soon, she informed the
Emperor that she had to return to Vienna, out of
deference to her father's wishes. As though a
wife's first duty were not to obey her husband!
But already her evil genius was active at her side:
Neipperg, the man who had been appointed to
escort her to Vienna, in the capacity of *chevalier
d'honneur*. That letter, written on August 10th,
was the last the Emperor received.

On August 18th he was beginning to grow

anxious. Among the numbered letters he received, some numbers, he observed, were missing; it was clear that his wife's correspondence was being watched and intercepted. And her silence rankled in his heart.

Yet he had not abandoned hope. Madame Mère, Laetitia Bonaparte, was at his side; and who better than a mother can console a sorrowing soul? He expected his wife to come at the season of the grape-harvest, looked forward to acquainting her with the mixture of white wine and herbs known in the island as *vermouth*. With the arrival of Princess Pauline Borghèse, *née* Bonaparte, there would be quite a family gathering. And Napoleon made pilgrimages to the shrine of the Madonna di Marciana, on Monte Giove, whence he could see, far off on the horizon, his native island, Corsica.

ISLAND OF ELBA 18 *Aug.*

Ma bonne Louise

I have written to you frequently; I presume you have done the same, yet I have received none of your letters since the one written within a few days of your departure from Vienna. I have had no news of my son. Such conduct is very stupid and atrocious. Madame is here and in good health; her accommodation is good. My health is good. Your apartments are ready for you, and I look forward to seeing you in September for the vintage. No one has any right to stand in the way of your coming. I have written to you on the point. So mind you come. I am awaiting you with impatience. You are aware of all the sentiments I bear you. I will write nothing more to-day, as this letter may not reach you. Princess Pauline will be here in the middle of September.

This is your Saint's Day, I send you my best wishes. Complain of their behaviour to you, in preventing a woman and a child from writing to me. Such behaviour is despicable. Adio, mio bene.

NAP.

Ma bonne amie

I have received your letter No. 19, dated August 10th. I presume you have received mine since. I was glad to hear Corvisart was with you. I am here in a hermitage, about 2,000 feet above sea level, overlooking the Mediterranean on all sides, and in the midst of a forest of chestnut trees. The spot is a very pleasant one. My health is very good. I spend part of the day shooting; I long to see you, and also my son. I shall be glad to see Isabei [Isabey]. There are some very fine landscapes to be drawn, here. Adieu, ma bonne Louise. Tout à toi. Ton

NAP.

LA MADONNA DI MARCIANO 28 *Aug.*

Many thanks for what you sent me.

"I am impatiently awaiting you." The woman who came to visit the exile in his solitude, on September 1st, was his mistress of a day, Countess Walewska, with her son. But what was Marie-Louise doing?

Aix-en-Savoie, where she received her husband's pleading letters—Aix-les-Bains, where Marie-Louise was recuperating—stands like a frontier boundary-post, marking a turning-point of history. "I intend to return to Vienna about the beginning of October", she writes to her bosom friend, Victoire de Poutet. "Try to stay on till then. This spa has benefited my health; I take the baths regularly, and they have done my chest a great deal of good." Of Napoleon she has ceased to speak.

Far from going to join her husband, she returned once more to her father's palace. "Do come back to see the recluses of Schönbrunn", she writes to her friend, "for really we deserve that name, considering the way we live here in the midst of a gay crowd intent on fêtes and dancing, whose only care is to amuse themselves."

If we are to believe a scrap of gossip retailed by Charlotte de Sor, Napoleon was talked of in the Viennese court of those days as "the gentleman at Elba".

But a day dawned when the "gentleman at Elba" was once again "the Emperor".

From the *Inconstant*—so aptly named—he landed on the shore of Golfe Juan, on March 1st, 1815. His progress to the capital was one long ovation. On March 12th, at Lyons, he wrote to Marie-Louise; Méneval has recorded the gist of his letter. "Summoned by the French nation, I have answered their appeal. Everywhere I have been greeted with enthusiasm. In a few days I shall be in Paris. I count on you and my son to meet me there at the end of the month."

Marie-Louise was flustered, unable to make up her mind. "One day she told me she would not go back to France, because she could not see the least hope of peace for the country. Next day she said that, if the Emperor would give up his schemes of conquest and reign peacefully, she had reason to think that no obstacle would be put in the way of her return to France and she felt no distaste for living there again, as she had always had a liking for the French." Such were the statements made by her to Baron Méneval.

But the *chevalier d'honneur* whom the Austrian Emperor had assigned to her—General Neipperg—was at her side. On April 11th, writing to her friend Victoire de Poutet, she deplores his departure. "Now I have absolutely no one to advise me; in my present situation, and considering my age, I still need somebody of the kind." In May she writes again: "I have not seen anything of General Neipperg for the last eighteen days." So she has come to the stage of counting the days!

Napoleon's messengers found the frontiers of Austria closed to them. Montrond, who managed to get through, thanks to an episcopal passport, informed Méneval with a smile—we may be sceptical about the "smile"—that he had been given a free hand . . . to kidnap the Empress disguised as a man.

"I cannot say when the Empress will go to France", Méneval admitted on April 7th, 1815, in a secret answer to a message from Napoleon. Indeed, her feelings had been worked on to such an extent that the Empress was terrified at the thought of returning to France. During the past six months everything possible had been done to estrange her from her husband. "Last Sunday, when I was dining with the Empress, alone, Her

Majesty told me that she had come to an irrevocable decision: never to return to the Emperor."

On April 13th, a letter from Napoleon reached Vienna, but as it was intercepted, Marie-Louise was given only a summary of its contents by word of mouth. Nevertheless, another letter, the last of all, reached her hands: it was Méneval who transmitted it. Marie-Louise refused to read it. "I have sworn to hand over everything to my father", she explained to her secretary, a dependable man whom the Emperor had appointed to her service.

Méneval, who had so nobly carried out his mission, despite "a cloud of loathsome spies", was compelled to leave Vienna. On May 12th, the Allies declared war on France. Méneval bade good-bye to the little King of Rome, telling him he was going back to France and would see his father there. "Monsieur Méra, please tell him I love him as much as ever", the poor child said; he looked "sad as one of those victims of old times who were led forth to sacrifice, garlanded with flowers." "I realize that from now on all relations between myself and France are at an end"—such was the farewell message of Marie-Louise—"but I shall never forget my adopted land. Tell the Emperor I wish him well. I hope he will understand the unfortunate position in which I am placed. I will never countenance a divorce, but I ask him to consent to a separation."

The Battle of Waterloo, on June 18th, and the Emperor's exile to St. Helena, the Ultima Thule of despair, served as an acid test of the sincerity

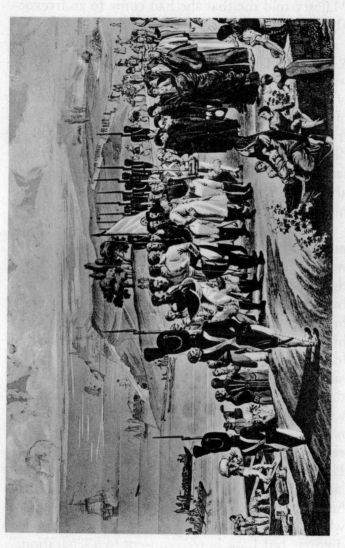

THE ARRIVAL AT ELBA
May 4th, 1814.

*From the picture by Sir Charles Eastlake
in the Lansdowne Collection.*

THE END OF A GREAT STORY

Napoleon standing at the gangway of H.M.S. Bellerophon,
Plymouth Sound, 1815.

of her feelings. Marie-Louise was at Baden when she heard the news that the Emperor was taken prisoner. The mistress of the house where she was staying, Marquise Scarampy, danced with joy, while the servants, who had an almost fanatical devotion for Napoleon, were prostrated with grief. The Marquise sent a note to Marie-Louise—whose door was always closed to visitors till eleven o'clock—telling her the news. "Thank you— but I knew about it already. I was thinking of a ride to Merkenstein. Do you think the weather's fine enough to risk it?"

Adam Albert de Neipperg was, we may take it, sure to be included in the party. "What do you think about it, General? What's your idea, General?"—such words were constantly on her lips, so the Baronne du Montet tells us. And such was the vanity of this dandy with the bandaged forehead, a one-eyed Don Juan who, in earlier days, had run away with a married woman, Thérèse Pois, at Mantua, that he was now aspiring to the conquest of Marie-Louise. "Within six months I shall be her lover, and very soon her husband. . . . Marie-Louise is charming, pretty as a rose."

In the *entourage* of the ex-Empress, Napoleon's name was taboo. The French staff had been disbanded, and replaced by German servants. The past was dead, its memory in oblivion. In the heart of Marie-Louise we can detect no trace of that generous compassion which is a woman's appanage, and might well have been accorded to one of the greatest griefs, the most pitiable disasters, the world has ever known. No, not a trace of it. . . .

In the prison-house of St. Helena, to the anguish that captivity must mean for one who, in his time, was master of the world, was to be added now the cruellest of griefs that can befall a husband and a father: loneliness of heart.

Index

NOTE :—Numbers in heavier type indicate references in the newly discovered Letters of Napoleon.

Index

Bertrand, General, 150, 197, 198, 270, 277

Bessières, Marshal; Duke of Istria, 67, 148, 161

Bibliothéque Nationale, 15, 19, 115

Blücher, Field-Marshal, 138, 141, 184, 185, 187, 192, 197, 198, 203, 205, 213, 217, 218, 233, 234, 236, 247

Bonaparte, Caroline, Queen of Naples, 23, 27, 29, 30, 42, 128, 233

Bonaparte, Elisa [Bacciochi], Grand Duchess of Tuscany, 33, 34

Bonaparte, Jerome, King of Westphalia, 61, 67, 70, 81, 168, 255

Bonaparte, Joseph, King of Spain, 167, 172, 173, 205, 208, 209, 210, 223, 224, 226, 236, 237, 238, 239, 240, 241, 242, 249, 255

Bonaparte, Laetitia ("Madame Mère"), 255, 278

Bonaparte, Louis, King of Holland, 35, 63, 64, 201, 255

Bonaparte, Pauline (Princess Borghese), 27, 33, 37, 42, 43, 255, 271, 279

Borghèse, Prince Aldobrandini, 57

Borodino, 95, 96, 97, 98, 100, 107, 121

Breslau, 163, 184

Briare, 259, 261, 267, 268, 270

Brie-contre-Aubert, 229

Brienne, 205, 246, 247

C

Cadore, Duc de (see Champagny)

Cachot, M. Edouard, 13, 14

Cafarelli, General, 21, 172, 177, 179

Cain, M. Julien, 15

Cambacérès, Jean Jacques Regis de; Duke of Parma (Archchancellor), 125, 128, 138, 147, 162, 163, 173, 177, 181, 209, 237, 244

Carrara, 259

Castellane, 54, 59, 61

Castiglione, Duc de (see Augereau)

Castiglione, Duchesse de, 225, 226

Castlereagh, Lord, 230

Caulaincourt, Armand Augustin Louis, Marquis de; Duke of Vicenza, 38, 46, 81, 103, 113, 142, 156, 159, 160, 164, 176, 183, 221, 222, 245, 250, 252, 255, 259, 261, 263

Chalons, 81, 177, 179, 205, 208, 213, 217, 233, 240, 241, 247

Champagny, Jean Baptiste Nompère de; Duke of Cadore, 232, 252, 253

Châtillon-sur-Seine, Peace Conference, 211, 222, 228, 243

Cherbourg, 181, 182, 183, 184, 186, 187, 188, 191, 192

Compiègne, 15, 32, 33, 72, 81, 232

Corvisart (Dr.), 259, 260, 270, 272, 279

Court, Viennese, 27, 28

Court, French, 28, 47, 82, 84, 108

D

Danzig, 52, 53, 55, 56, 57, 62, 138, 143, 204

Davout, Marshal; Prince d'Eckmühl, 66, 70, 81, 87, 90, 113, 122, 123

Index

Index